George Thomas Brown

Dentition as Indicative of the Age of the Animals of the Farm

George Thomas Brown

Dentition as Indicative of the Age of the Animals of the Farm

ISBN/EAN: 9783337231484

Printed in Europe, USA, Canada, Australia, Japan

Cover: Foto ©Andreas Hilbeck / pixelio.de

More available books at **www.hansebooks.com**

DENTITION

AS INDICATIVE OF THE

AGE OF THE ANIMALS OF THE FARM.

BY

PROFESSOR G. T. BROWN, C.B.

FOURTH EDITION.

LONDON:

JOHN MURRAY, ALBEMARLE STREET.

1895.

SUMMARY OF CONTENTS.

————◦⟨⁕⟩◦————

DENTITION

AS INDICATIVE OF THE

AGE OF THE ANIMALS OF THE FARM.

———•◦•———

INTRODUCTORY.

JUDGING the age by the teeth is an ancient art, the origin of which may perhaps be dated back to the time of the domestication of the horse—an animal which, for commercial and economic reasons, must have attracted more attention than those which were used for food. In modern times the system was extended to other animals of the farm, as appears from the older veterinary writers on dentition, among them M. Girard, whose observations and illustrations were copied by Youatt, and from his book by more recent writers.

There is a general belief among stock-owners that the improvement which has taken place in the various breeds of farm animals, as the result of careful breeding and feeding, has led to early maturity of the teeth, as well as of other organs and tissues of the body. For this idea, Girard, and after him Youatt and other writers, are certainly responsible. According to them, cattle do not get the full set of broad teeth until they are four or five years old, sheep at four years old, and swine at three years old. But when the writer of this paper, with these views in his mind, commenced an inquiry on dentition in 1850, he soon found out how very wide of the truth they were. Cattle bred on the Royal Agricultural College Farm had their dentition perfectly complete in most cases under three years and a half, in many instances soon after three years, and, in one case, at two years and ten months. Sheep had their full complement of teeth at three years, and pigs soon after one year and a half. All the animals on the farm were of the average quality—

improved shorthorn cattle, Cotswold sheep, and Berkshire pigs. They were kept on liberal rations, but not forced for show purposes.

The inquiry was continued beyond the College Farm, and the cattle, sheep, and swine belonging to well-known breeders and exhibitors were examined, and it may be stated without hesitation, that from the commencement of the investigation to the present time, including a period of more than forty years, no remarkable advance has been observed in the rate of development of the teeth. None of the thousands of cattle, sheep, and pigs which have been examined during that period have shown examples of dental precocity more pronounced in character than those which were met with in the early part of the inquiry among the animals on the College Farm at Cirencester and elsewhere.

It did not at first occur to the writer to question the truth of the assumption that the improvement of the various breeds of farm stock by selection and high feeding sufficiently accounted for the early appearance of the teeth; but now, after a further period of forty years has elapsed, *i.e.* from 1850 to 1895, without any marked change in the development of the teeth—although breeders have been during the whole period steadily devoting their knowledge and energies to the cultivation of the various breeds of cattle, sheep, and swine—it is impossible to avoid the conclusion that the original version of the development of the teeth was based on imperfect observation.

With some exhibitors, the number of whom it may be observed grows less year by year, it is a favourite contention that the system of forcing animals by high feeding on prepared food facilitates the cutting of the teeth. Physiology affords no ground for the assertion, and experience proves that it is incorrect. The use of prepared food lessens the wear of the masticating organs, and rather tends to retard than accelerate their development.

DENTITION OF THE HORSE.

Among the animals of the farm, the horse has always occupied a prominent position, and everything relating to his management in health and disease has received special attention. It is not therefore remarkable that horsemen were familiar with the method of judging the animal's age by the teeth long before it was ascertained that a similar method was applicable to other farm-stock. And at the present time, although the investigations which have been carried out by veterinary authorities on the Continent and in this country have led to the collection of a large amount of valuable evidence in reference to the development of the teeth of the ox, sheep, and pig, the fact must be admitted that the teeth of the horse exhibit reliable indications of the age for a much longer period than those of any other animal.

The ages of cattle, sheep, and swine are to be judged with accuracy only during the period occupied by the cutting of the temporary teeth and their replacement by permanent organs; but a peculiar conformation of the teeth of the horse enables the expert to form an opinion of the animal's age long after the completion of permanent dentition. Girard carries his description of the changes which occur in the form of the tables of the incisor teeth, or more properly the nippers, up to the age of twenty years; and Mr. Sidney Galvayne, in his book on the age of the horse, gives the marks which indicate the age, according to his view, up to thirty years.

When dentition is completed, the horse has six incisors or nippers in the front of the mouth in both upper and lower jaws, and twenty-four molars, six on each side, in the jaw.

In the male there are also four tusks, one on each side of the upper and lower jaws, between the corner incisors and the molar teeth. Small conical teeth, known as wolves' teeth, appear in many instances in front of the first upper molars in the colt, and sometimes remain after the temporary are exchanged for permanent teeth; but, as merely rudimentary organs, they will not require any notice beyond the statement that a vulgar prejudice has assigned to them a special significance as a cause of blindness, and on this ground they are often punched out. If this operation is roughly done it is a mere act of cruelty; in any case it is superfluous. But, so far as the teeth are concerned, their retention or removal is a matter of indifference.

It is customary to judge the age by the incisor teeth, for the reason that they are more easily examined. The amateur may be content to form an opinion from the mere cursory inspection of the signs which are most readily observed; but the professional examiner is expected to take advantage of all the evidence which he can obtain by a critical inspection of molars and incisors, and it is a fact that in some animals at certain periods of dentition the molar teeth afford more certain indications of age than the incisors.

In the illustration on next page (Fig. 1) the temporary and permanent incisors of the horse are depicted side by side, and in each the following parts may be distinguished. First, the crown of the tooth which projects above the gum; the neck, which is encircled by the gum; and the fang, which is lodged in its appropriate socket in the jaw.

It will be observed that the temporary tooth is much smaller than the permanent organ, which is placed on the left hand, and also that the distinction between the upper part of the tooth, or crown, and the fang is much more marked in the milk-tooth. In fact, the permanent incisor does not indicate any actual line of separation between the upper and lower portions.

For all practical purposes a knowledge of the form of the

Fig. 1. – *Permanent and Temporary Incisors of Horse.*

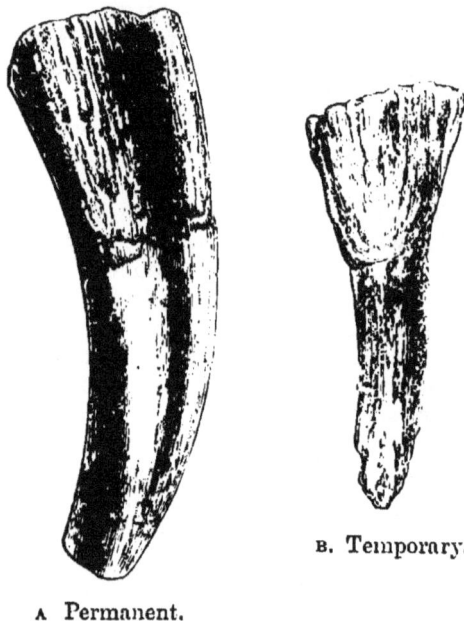

B. Temporary.

A Permanent.

teeth, and especially the signs which distinguish the temporary from the permanent organs, is quite sufficient. To the scientist, the study of the minute structure and development of the teeth, in their connection with the habits of the different classes of animals, is very interesting, but it does not assist the practical observer in judging the age.

The next illustration (Fig. 2) shows a perfectly formed central permanent incisor. All the parts of the tooth which the expert is required to note carefully are clearly defined in this figure.

Attention is, in the first place, directed to the upper surface of the crown of the incisor, which is described as the table of the tooth. In the centre of the table is a cavity (*a*) familiarly known as the "mark," on account of the dark colour of its interior.

In form, the table of the incisor tooth may be described as an elliptical figure, with its long axis running transversely. At the end of the fang the figure is also elliptical, but the long axis is exactly at right angles to that of the table; and by

Fig. 2.—*Permanent Incisor (Horse).*

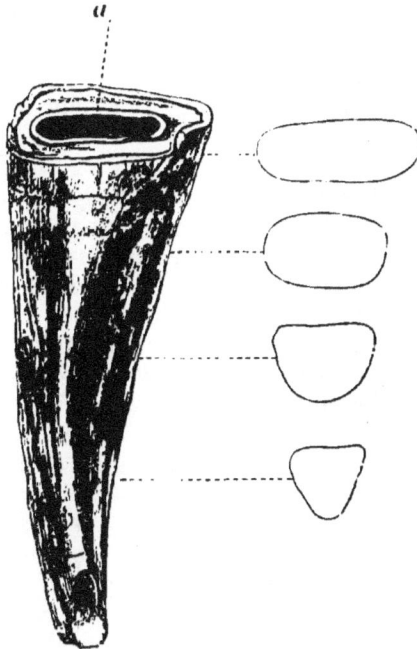

grinding, or by the slower process of wearing an incisor tooth from the upper surface towards the fang, a series of figures will be formed, passing from the elliptical to the oval, the square, and the triangle, first with equal sides, and then with two sides longer than the base.

For the purpose of making the nature of these changes evident, the outlines of the figures, which result from the wear of tooth structures, are placed on the right of the tooth (Fig. 2). There are, however, other points which require to be noticed. The cavity in the centre of the table is formed by an inflexion of the structures of the tooth in the shape of a hollow cone, the apex of which reaches into the fang. In the recent tooth the cavity extends quite across the table, but, necessarily, as the tooth is worn it becomes more and more circumscribed, and at length the apex of the hollow cone is reached, and the "mark" consists of a mere speck, and then is entirely obliterated.

Owing to the inflexion of the whole of the tooth-structures to form the hollow cone, the tables of the incisors have, besides the ivory and crusta, two distinct rings of enamel, which are distinguished from the other parts by their pearly whiteness— an external or larger ring which forms the outline of the table, and a central ring which surrounds the cavity in the centre of the table. That part of the tooth which is situated in the front of the mark is described as the anterior edge, and the portion behind it as the posterior edge.

All these parts are indicated in the diagram (Fig. 2), and it is necessary that the reader should clearly recognise them, in order to understand the description of the changes which are occasioned by the wear to which the teeth are subjected.

While the temporary dentition is proceeding, and also during the time that the permanent are taking the places of the temporary teeth, the examiner may form an opinion of the age by merely noting what teeth are in the mouth; but when these changes are completed, he is compelled to base his conclusion upon the evidence which he gains from an inspection of the tables of the incisor teeth, those of the lower jaw being generally selected. In doing this, he has to observe whether the cavity or mark extends across the tooth, or is surrounded by a line of worn structure, in which case the table is said to be fully formed, as it appears in Fig. 2. The width of the worn surface in front of the cavity, as compared with that at the back, should be taken into consideration, and also the shape of the table, whether oval, or square, or triangular.

No particular importance can be attached to the tusks as a means of judging the age. They only occur in the horse, and are less regular than the other teeth in the time of their eruption. The small rudimentary teeth which sometimes exist in place of tusks in the mare need not be taken into account at all.

There may in certain cases be reason to suspect that the mouth of the horse under examination has been manipulated, with the view to make the animal appear younger or older than it really is. Up to the age of five years it may be advantageous to the seller to convince the purchaser that the horse is above its real age; but as six years old is, according to general conviction, the period of equine perfection, an old horse gains by being made to appear as near that age as possible.

That the horse's mouth is sometimes subjected to certain operations for the purpose of deception cannot be doubted. Many young animals come into the market showing by the malposition of their teeth, or the absence of some of them altogether, that violence has been employed to aid the natural process of eruption, but often in so bungling a manner that the object has been defeated. Early extraction of the temporary teeth facilitates the cutting of the permanent organs, and by commencing with the central incisors as soon as signs of their displacement are seen, and continuing the same system in respect of the lateral and corner teeth, the whole of the permanent incisors may be brought into the mouth soon after four years. The cutting of the tusks at this age is also facilitated by fitting a hot iron, cunningly arranged, over the points of the teeth which may be just pricking through the gum, and thus burning away the structure which obscured the organs from view.

It was a favourite argument with Mayhew, who devoted much time to the study of dentition, and certainly was the first to announce the fact of the cutting of the first and second permanent molars in the same year, instead of following each other at an interval of a year—as had been taught previously—that extraction of the temporary teeth, or lancing the gums, or the adoption of any means by which inflammation was excited, would tend rather to retard than facilitate the advance of the permanent teeth. Mr. Mayhew's contention was, that during the existence of inflammation blood was determined to the gum, and therefore a less than the ordinary supply was sent to the new tooth, which would consequently be developed slowly. However satisfactory this explanation might be to the physiologist, it had no weight with the breeder, who knew from practical experience that the permanent or second teeth did come up more quickly if the first teeth were taken out.

Treated in the manner above described, the horse at four years off is accepted as a five-year-old; but the expert is well aware that at the age of four years there are eight molar teeth which have only just approached the level of the others, and these enable him to distinguish with absolute certainty between a horse of four and another of five years old.

The clumsy expedient of excavating the centres of the teeth of old horses, and blackening the cavity thus made by means of a hot iron to represent the lost mark, is not likely to deceive any one who is familiar with the anatomy of the teeth; and the operation which is dignified by the term " Bishoping," from the name of its inventor, is too laborious to be often performed. Indeed, it may be allowed that the tricks which are played with horses' mouths are not so frequent or so successful as to constitute an important element in the question of the value of the evidence of age which is afforded by the teeth.

It is customary to calculate the ages of all thoroughbreds from January 1, and of other horses from May 1. The terms " off" and " coming " are employed with the understanding that they mean the addition to or subtraction from the stated age of a few months. Thus "three years off " means three years and about three months; and " coming four years " means that the horse wants about three months to complete the year. It is not essential that the examiner should conform to usage in respect of the terms above mentioned, unless he thinks fit to accept them; nor is he compelled to insist that the year shall be completed in all cases on the 1st of January or May. The statement of the opinion of a horse's age will be made absolutely, and without any reference to an arbitrary standard, which nevertheless may, for ordinary purposes, have a certain amount of convenience.

In reference to horses which are exhibited in different classes at Shows, a question has more than once arisen as to the precise meaning or intention of the terms applying to the class, and the question has not yet been answered in a satisfactory manner. For example, an animal entered in the four-year-old class has a condition of dentition which indicates that he is nearly five years old. This may be admitted by the exhibitor, but he also contends that the horse is a four-year-old until he has reached his fifth birthday. If this plea be allowed, it is obvious that a horse foaled in the beginning of the year may have to compete with one which was foaled late in the same year.

Evidence of the Age of the Horse during Temporary and Permanent Dentition.

At *birth* the foal has the two central temporary incisors somewhat laterally placed, in consequence of the jaw not being wide enough to accommodate them both in front. The teeth are nearly covered by the gum, and only a small portion of the upper anterior edges is to be seen. In some cases the extreme corners of the lateral incisors are to be detected in outline under the gum. The three temporary molars are usually under the gum at the time of birth. The state of the incisors at birth is shown in the following drawing (Fig. 3), which was taken, on the morning of its birth, from a cart-colt foaled at the Royal Agricultural College Farm.

By the end of the *second week after birth*, the central incisors will be fairly in the mouth, and in *six or eight weeks* the lateral teeth, and also the temporary molars, are well up.

In the illustration on p. 12 (Fig. 4) the state of the incisor teeth at *two months* old is shown. The central incisors at this age have the surfaces very slightly worn, and the cavity or infundibulum is not surrounded by a line of worn structure; only the anterior edges of the teeth have yet been subject to attrition. In the lateral incisors the wear is confined to a small portion of

Fig. 3.—*Incisors of Colt at birth.*

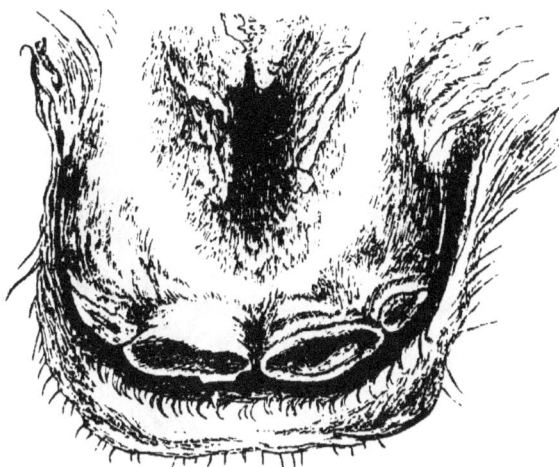

the anterior edge which is nearest to the central teeth. These appearances are indicated in the drawing (Fig. 4).

Between *two and six months* old the central and lateral incisors increase in size with the growth of the animal. At *six months* old the mouth has a very neat and compact appearance. The centrals and laterals are well developed, and their anterior edges are worn level. The posterior edges are, however, still rather below the anterior, and the table, therefore, is not perfectly formed. The drawing on p. 13 (Fig. 5) was taken from the mouth of a cart-colt at the age of six months.

Soon after *seven months*, indications of the cutting of the corner teeth may often be seen, and in many instances the points of the teeth will be observed pricking through the gum.

At *nine months* old the colt will have the corner incisors in the mouth with their extreme anterior edges in apposition, leaving a triangular space, which is seen most perfectly on a side view when the lips are slightly separated.

At this period the fourth molar, which is a permanent tooth from the first, begins to protrude through the gum, and by the time of the completion of the first year it is level with the temporary molars; but its surface is not worn, and the recent appearance of the tooth is most important as evidence of the age of one year.

The illustration on p. 14 (Fig. 6) shows the condition of the molar teeth at the completion of the *first year*. Three temporary molars have the upper surface worn, and are thus readily

Fig. 4.— *Incisors of Colt at two months.*

distinguished from the fourth molar, which has only recently been cut.

The illustration on p. 15 (Fig. 7) shows the shell-like character of the corner teeth, and the state of the tables of the other incisors in the *one-year-old* colt; and it may be remarked that the appearances correspond with those of the teeth of the five-year-old horse; the chief difference being that in the yearling the teeth are temporary, and in the five-year-old permanent, organs.

A practical horseman would perhaps feel amused at the idea of the possibility of a yearling being taken for a five-year-old, or a two-year-old for a six; but in the case of rough forest-ponies, in which the aspect of colthood is quickly lost, such mistakes have occurred, and it is therefore not out of place to suggest that care should be taken to discriminate between the temporary incisors, and, if necessary, to refer to the molar teeth, in order to avoid such embarrassing blunders.

Under ordinary circumstances it will be more frequently necessary to distinguish between a yearling and a two-year-old, than between a one-year-old and a five, and it fortunately happens that at the age of *two years* another molar, the fifth in situation, is in the mouth, and may be at once distinguished by its recent appearance. Soon after eighteen months the fifth molar begins to protrude through the gum, and by the termination of the second year is level with the other molars, as shown in Fig. 8 (p. 16), so that any doubt which may remain after an inspection of the incisors may be settled by reference to the condition of the molars.

Fig. 5.—*Incisors of Colt at six months.*

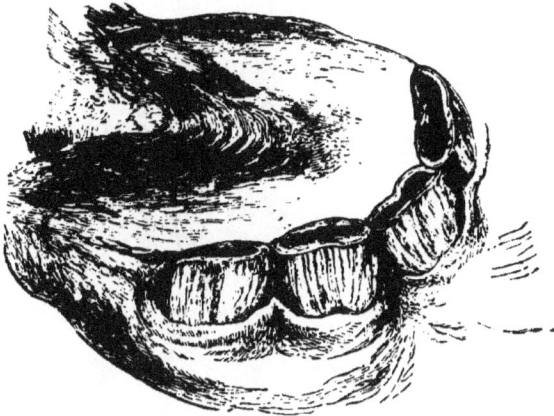

It will be observed in the figure just referred to that the surfaces of four molars are worn level, while the points of the new tooth, the fifth in position, are rounded, excepting a small portion at the inner side of the tooth, which shows the effects of attrition, but only to a slight extent.

The incisor teeth at two years of age have their tables perfectly formed as a rule ; but, in some instances, the corner teeth, although they have lost their shell-like character, still have a portion of the posterior edge untouched, as shown in the illustration of the mouth of a two-year-old filly (Fig. 9, p. 17).

Between two and three years of age the central temporary incisors of the horse are changed for permanent teeth, and the different phases of the change are sufficiently well defined to assist the examiner in deciding whether the animal is two years "off" or coming three years.

At two years "off," or *two years and a quarter*, there will be

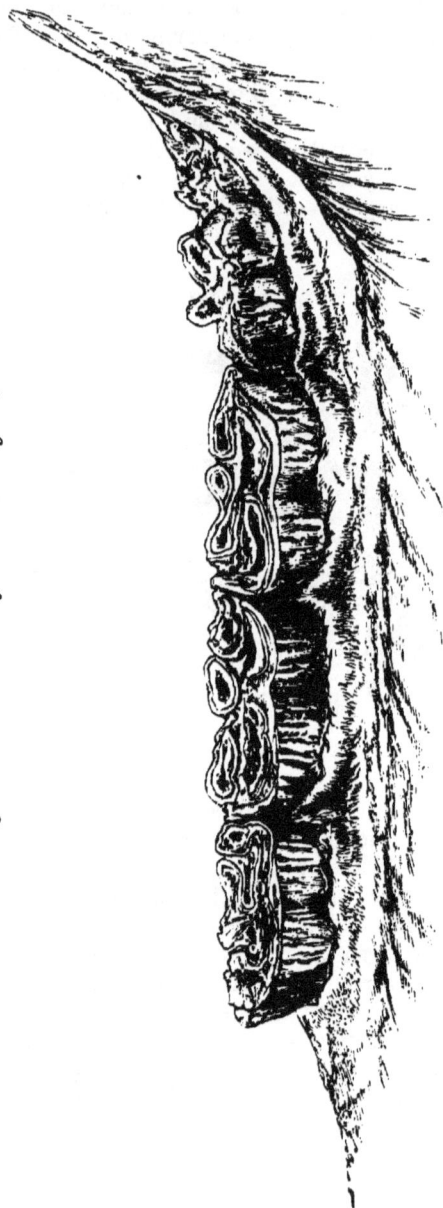

Fig. 6.—*Molar Teeth of Colt at one year.*

evident signs of the shedding of the upper central incisors.
The gum at the necks of the teeth is somewhat sunken, and the
colour is rather deeper than in other parts. Very soon a red
line appears in this position, and it is evident that one or both
of the temporary teeth are only held in their places by a small
portion of the fang which has not yet been absorbed. At two
years and a half the permanent teeth will generally be in the
mouth. Perhaps one temporary central incisor may yet remain ;
but even in that case the state of the permanent teeth will be
sufficient evidence of the animal's age.

Fig. 7.—*Incisors of Colt at one year.*

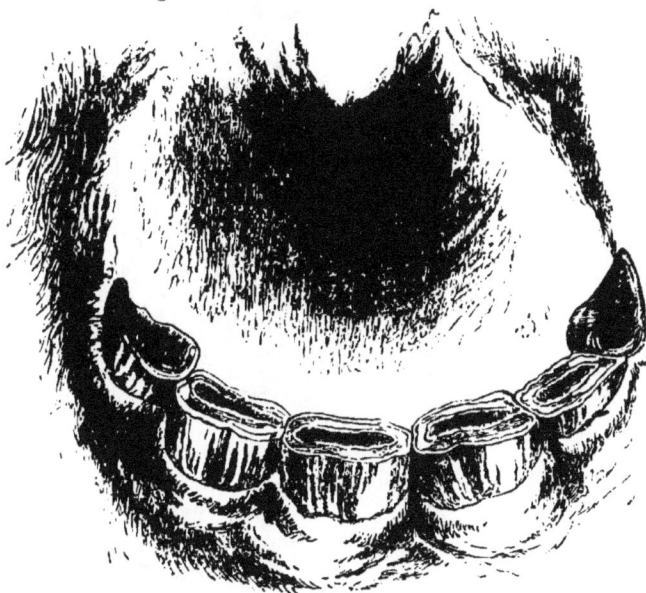

The mouth of the horse at *two years and a half* has a very
characteristic appearance, especially when viewed in the front
by separating the lips. The four permanent central incisors
are seen in position about half grown, with deep cavities or
infundibula extending across each tooth, presenting a striking
contrast to the worn temporary teeth on each side of them.
The new permanent teeth at this age are not more than half-
way up, and there is consequently a considerable space between
the upper and lower teeth when the temporary teeth are in
apposition.

When the horse has reached the age of *two years and nine*

Fig. 8.—*Molars of Colt at two years.*

months, the four permanent incisors will be in actual contact, at least in regard to their anterior edges when the mouth is closed; but on examining the tables it is apparent that no wear has taken place, and the posterior edges of the teeth are not yet level with the anterior.

At *three years* old the central permanent incisors are fully developed, and the anterior edges show a narrow line of worn surface. The posterior edges are level with the anterior, but are not worn to the same extent.

Fig. 9.—*Incisors of Cart-filly at two years.*

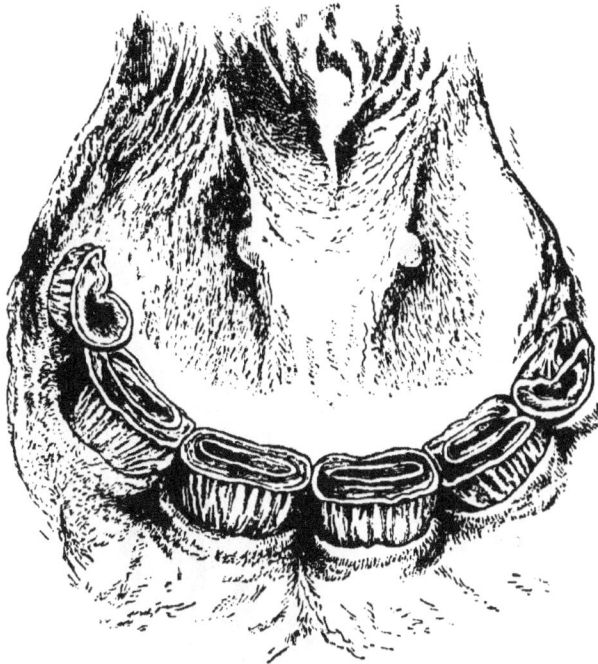

In giving an opinion in a case of dispute as to the age exceeding or not exceeding three years, the examiner will pay particular attention to the upper surfaces of the central permanent incisors in the first place. The tables of these teeth are not fully formed at three years of age, and the cavity is not bounded by a line of worn structure, but extends quite across the teeth, and is open at least on one side and sometimes on both sides. Perfectly formed tables on the central incisors will certainly indicate that the horse is above the age of three, and

B

it is most probable that the state of the lateral temporary incisors will show that they are about to be shed, a fact which will add materially to the evidence.

These appearances of the incisors are shown in the next illustration (Fig. 10), which was taken from the mouth of a colt on the completion of the third year. No difficulty ought to be found in recognising the three-year-old mouth at a glance. The fully developed permanent incisors are seen in striking

Fig. 10.—*Incisors of Horse at three years.*

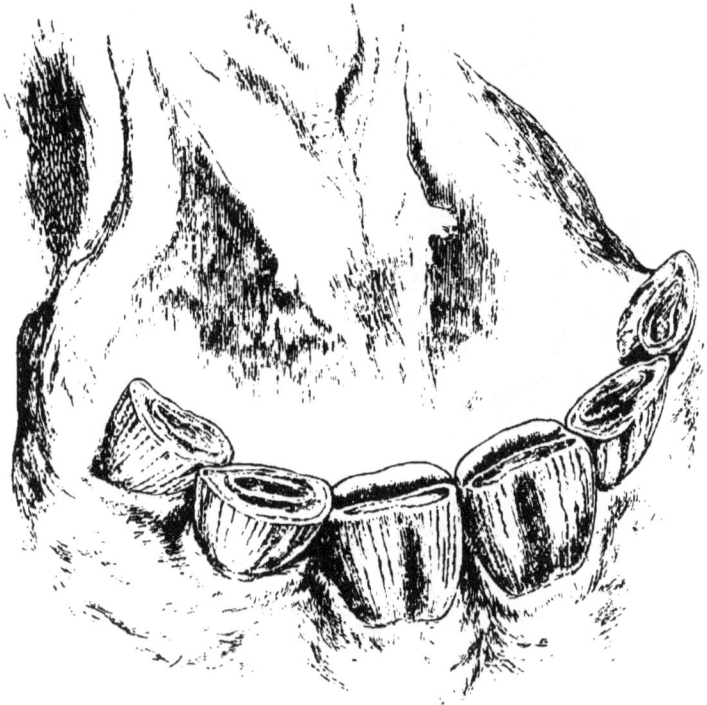

contrast to the temporary teeth on each side of them, and cannot easily be overlooked.

During the development of the central permanent incisors in the course of the third year, an important change is going on in the first and second molars, the fangs of which are gradually absorbed as the permanent teeth push their way up underneath them.

It has already been stated that these teeth do not follow the rule by coming up singly at intervals of a year, but advance nearly together, so that eight molars are cut between the second and third year.

At two years and a half old, one or two of the permanent molars may be in the mouth. Sometimes the second in position is cut before the first, and a careful examination will show that the crowns of the first and second temporary molars which yet remain are only retained in their position by a slight attachment to the gum, and very little force is required to dislodge them.

The drawing on p. 20 (Fig. 11) shows the condition of the molar teeth soon after two years and a half. A permanent tooth, the first in position, is seen occupying the place of the temporary molar which has fallen, and the second permanent tooth is pushing its way up under the second temporary molar, which is only held in its place by small portions of the fangs that have not yet been absorbed. The fifth molar, which was up at two years old, is fully developed, and is quite clear from the angle of the jaw.

At three years old the first and second permanent molars are well up, and the top and bottom teeth are in contact when the mouth is closed ; but the teeth are distinguished by the recent appearance which they present in comparison with the worn surfaces of the teeth immediately behind them.

From the completion of the third year to the termination of the fourth year, the changes which have been described in reference to the central incisors and the first and second molars occur in the lateral incisors, and the third and sixth molars.

At three years " off" the same condition of the gum which was described in respect of the upper central temporary incisors now appears at the necks of the lower lateral temporary incisors. At *three years and a half* some, or perhaps all four, of the permanent lateral incisors are in the mouth ; and soon afterwards the third and sixth permanent molars are cut, as shown in the drawing (Fig. 12, p. 20).

No difficulty would be experienced in distinguishing the recent molars in the condition represented in the illustration. The first and second, and the fourth and fifth molars show considerable wear, while the new teeth present rounded points on their surfaces, and are not nearly level with the other teeth. One or two of the most projecting points of the sixth molars show the effects of attrition ; but these teeth at the age of three years and a half have their posterior points close to the angle of the jaw and still covered with the gum.

At *four years* old the horse has the lateral permanent incisors in apposition, and the third and sixth molars are level, or nearly level, with the other teeth.

Fig. 11.—Molars of Horse at two years and seven months.

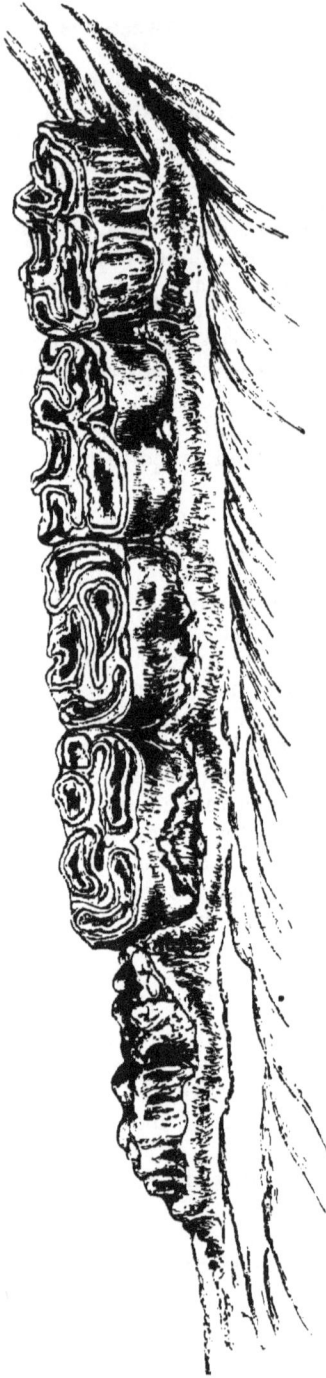

Fig. 12.—Molars of Horse at three years and eight months.

The tusks of the horse are often through the gums at four years of age, but they are not usually fully developed before five years, and occasionally they are not well up before five years and a half. As a means of judging the age, these teeth are of little importance.

Fig. 13.—*Incisors of Horse at four years.*

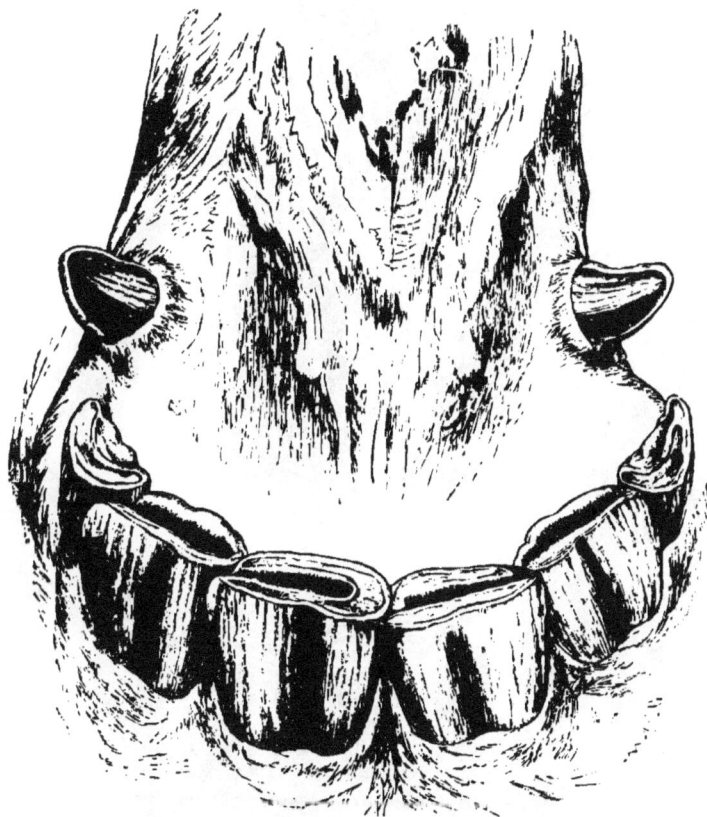

The above drawing (Fig. 13) represents the state of the incisor teeth on the completion of the fourth year.

Between *four and five years* the corner temporary incisors are removed, and the permanent teeth occupy their places. Indications of the change are seen at four years off in the upper corner incisors, and in a few months the temporary teeth are displaced, and the permanent organs are in the mouth. But their edges do not meet until the fifth year is completed, and even then the contact is limited to the anterior part, and a triangular space, similar to that which can be seen between the upper and lower corner teeth in the mouth of the yearling, may be recognised when the lips are separated at the side of the

Fig. 14.—*Incisors of Horse at five years.*

mouth.   The shell-like character of the corner permanent teeth is the special indication of five years old.

In the above figure (Fig. 14) the condition of the incisors in the five-year-old mouth is shown.

In the illustration it is evident that the corner permanent incisors show but slight indications of wear on the completion of the fifth year, only the anterior edge exhibiting the effects of attrition. The tables of the lateral incisors are fully formed by the central cavity being surrounded by a line of worn surface. In the central incisors the cavity has become extremely shallow.

The development of the corner permanent incisors completes the permanent dentition of the horse.

Indications of Age of the Horse afforded by the Teeth after the Completion of Permanent Dentition.

The horse occupies an exceptional position among the animals of the farm in respect to the evidence of age which is afforded by the teeth after all the permanent organs are developed, and there is no longer anything to be gained by a comparison between them and the temporary. All animals exhibit distinct signs of wear in their teeth as age advances ; but, owing to the peculiar arrangement of the structures of which the teeth are formed, the horse alone gives definite evidence which can be interpreted by a careful observer up to an advanced period of the animal's life.

It was explained in the preliminary observations on the teeth of the horse that the permanent incisors present two somewhat oval surfaces, one at the upper part of the tooth and the other at the end of the fang : the long axis of the first being horizontal, and that of the second vertical ; and, as a consequence, the wear of the tooth, from the upper towards the lower oval, results in a series of figures, some of which are depicted on page 7.

After five years, evidence of age is to be obtained by the inspection of the tables of the incisor teeth, in regard to their form, the extent and depth of the central cavity, and the form of the central enamel.

At *six years* old the horse's age is judged chiefly by the amount of wear which the corner teeth have sustained, although there are other marks that are worthy of notice.

The corner teeth have lost their shell-like character, and a line of worn surface surrounds the central cavity, excepting a small point where the corners touch the lateral incisors. The line of wear is broader at the anterior than at the posterior edge, and the cavity is still of considerable depth.

In the lateral incisors the cavity (or mark) is shallow, and much smaller than that of the corner incisors. The figure described by the central enamel is approaching an oval. The cavity in the central incisor is almost worn out, but its bound-

aries are distinctly marked by the central enamel which surrounds
it, forming an elliptical figure which extends almost across the
tooth in the direction of its long diameter, and is nearer to the
posterior than to the anterior edge.

The tusks are usually well developed, but their points are
not worn, and the hollows on their inner surfaces are well
defined.

Fig. 15.—*Incisors of Horse at six years.*

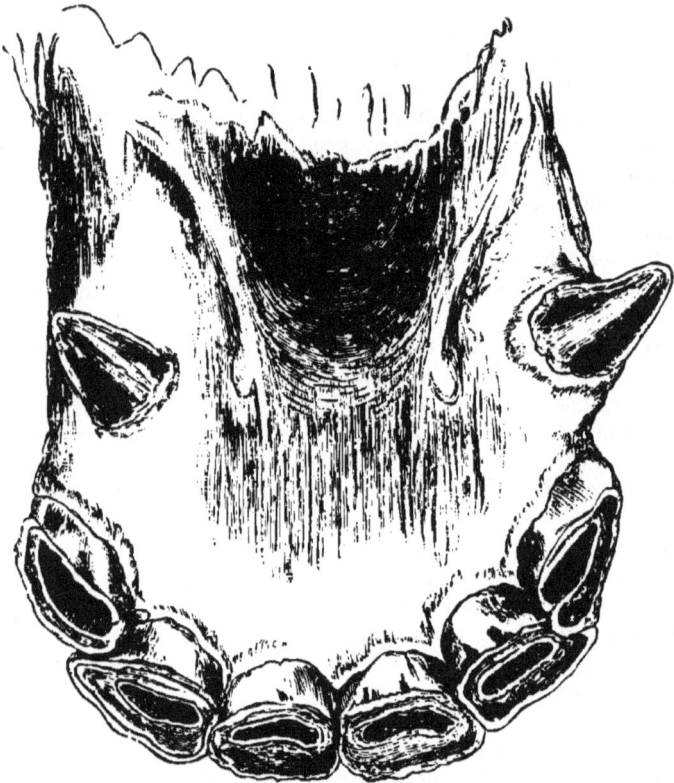

All the above characters are shown in the illustration
(Fig. 15) of the lower incisors of a six-year-old horse.

At *seven years* old the tables of the corner teeth are perfectly
formed, and the cavity in each tooth is very shallow. The
central enamel, however, is well defined and forms an elliptical
figure, which is nearer to the posterior than to the anterior edge
of the tooth. In the lateral incisors the central enamel forms a
figure which is nearer to the oval than to the elliptical, and the
mark, which is very shallow, does not extend so far across the

table of the tooth as it does at six years old. These teeth are also deeper from front to back than they were at six years.

The central incisors at seven years old have their sides elongated, so that the table approaches the figure of a triangle. The mark is very close to the posterior edge of the tooth, and the central enamel forms an oval with flattened sides in place of the elliptical figure which is shown in the drawing of the six-year-old mouth. The tusks are somewhat blunted at their points.

Fig. 16.—*Incisors of Horse at seven years.*

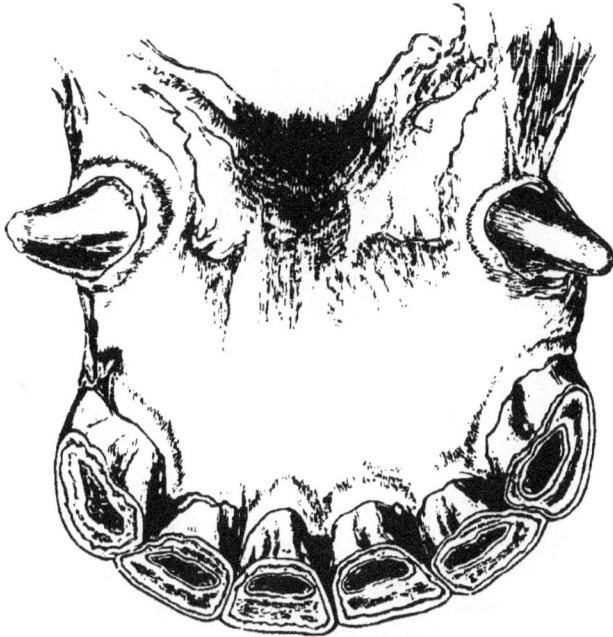

The above illustration (Fig. 16) represents the above-described characters of the seven-year-old mouth.

Between the seven-year-old and the eight-year-old mouth the difference at first sight is not very marked, and the examiner is required to look rather critically at the tables of the incisor teeth, the shape of the central enamel in the central incisors, and the form of the tables of the corner teeth.

In some cases the corner teeth will show almost as much wear at seven years old as they do in other cases at eight years; but there are differences in the height of the teeth above the gums and in the general aspect of the mouth, which must not be lost sight of when an accurate opinion has to be formed.

In the *eight-year-old* mouth the form of the tables of the incisors and the shape of the central enamel in the central incisor afford tolerably satisfactory indications of the age. The central teeth are more distinctly triangular than they were at seven years; the central enamel in these teeth is also triangular in figure. All the tables of the incisors are worn as level as the

Fig. 17.—*Incisors of Horse* (*"Peep-o'-day Boy"*) *at eight years.*

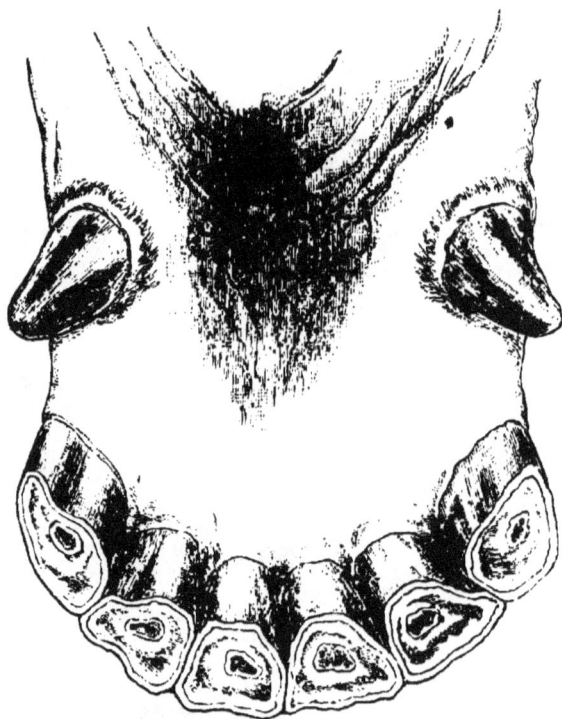

different degrees of density of the various structures will permit. The cavities are either very shallow, or quite obliterated by being filled up with one of the tooth tissues, although the central enamel in each tooth is perfectly well defined. The gum of the corner incisors at eight years has lost its circular form and become square. The tusks are more blunted at the tops than in the seven-year-old mouth.

In the above illustration (Fig. 17) the appearance of the eight-year-old mouth is shown. The drawing was copied from the mouth of " Peep-o'-day Boy " in 1852. The horse was foaled in 1844.

From *eight to ten years* old the changes occasioned by the wear to which the teeth have been subjected are not sufficiently regular to enable the examiner to speak positively as to the exact age, but during this period the cavity in each lower central incisor is worn out, and only a small circle of enamel in the tables of the central incisors remains to indicate its position. In the corner teeth at ten years old the central enamel has

Fig. 18.—*Incisors of Mare (" Solace ") at ten years.*

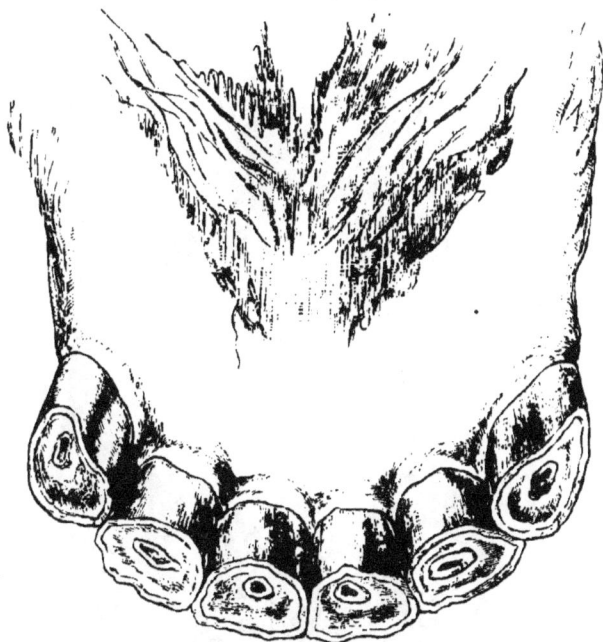

become round, or nearly so, as shown in the above drawing (Fig. 18) of the mouth of " Solace," a steeplechase mare, foaled in 1842. The teeth are depicted exactly as they appeared in the summer of 1852, and fairly represent the characters of the ten-year-old mouth.

At the age of ten years further evidence may, if necessary, be obtained by referring to the groove at the upper part of the corner incisor in the top jaw. At page 5 it was stated that Mr. Sidney Galvayne's system of judging the age of the horse proposes to define the age up to thirty years. The method, as will appear further on, consists chiefly in observing the length of the groove which appears in the upper corner incisor at ten years, and gradually extends to the lower edge of the tooth. In Fig. 22, page 31, the appearance of this groove at ten years old is shown.

At *twelve years* old the teeth are longer from the receding of the gums, and are also narrower in consequence of having been worn towards the fang, which decreases in width from the neck of the tooth to its termination. The tusks are blunted, especially

Fig. 19.—*Incisors of Horse ("Lothario") at twelve.*

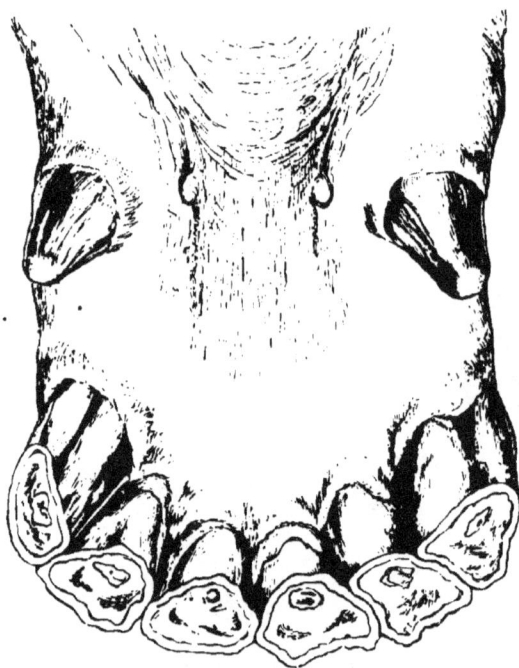

those of the upper jaw, and a quantity of tartar often surrounds those in the lower jaw. The incisors at this age project almost in a straight line from the jaws, and in some mouths a line drawn transversely across the tables of the teeth will cut the centres of all of them, excepting those of the corner teeth.

The above drawing (Fig. 19) represents the teeth of the thoroughbred horse "Lothario," foaled in 1840, as they appeared in 1852.

On comparing the tables of the teeth with those of the mare

"Solace" (Fig. 18) at the age of ten years, it will be seen that there are certain important differences. The central incisors have quite lost the "mark," which is only represented by a dot. The central enamel in the remaining incisors forms a much smaller figure than in the ten-year-old teeth. The corner teeth have become more oval in form, and only a trace of the central enamel can be seen.

After twelve or fourteen years of age, the evidence which is afforded by the tables of the teeth is not definite enough to justify a positive opinion as to the animal's age, and the illustra-

Fig. 20.—*Incisors of Horse ("Kremlin") at nineteen.*

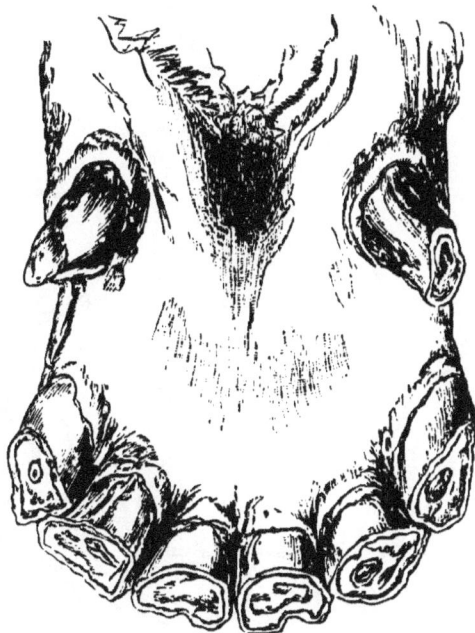

tions (Figs. 20, 21), which are accurate representations of the teeth of the thoroughbreds "Kremlin" and "Epirus," will show how far the appearances may differ in animals of the same age. Both horses were foaled in 1834, and the drawings show the state of the teeth in 1853, when the animals were nineteen years old.

In both cases the teeth form a more acute angle with the jaw than is usual at this age. In this particular both mouths agree, but in other respects they differ from each other to a noteworthy extent.

The mouth of " Kremlin " was drawn as a very remarkable specimen, and it may be said in regard to it that experienced judges have more than once decided that the teeth indicate the animal to be much above the actual age.

About the time that the cast of the mouth of " Kremlin " was taken, a specimen of a horse which was believed to be thirty-six years old at the time of his death was obtained, and it was observed that, so far as the tables of the teeth were concerned,

Fig. 21. — *Incisors of Horse (" Epirus ") at nineteen.*

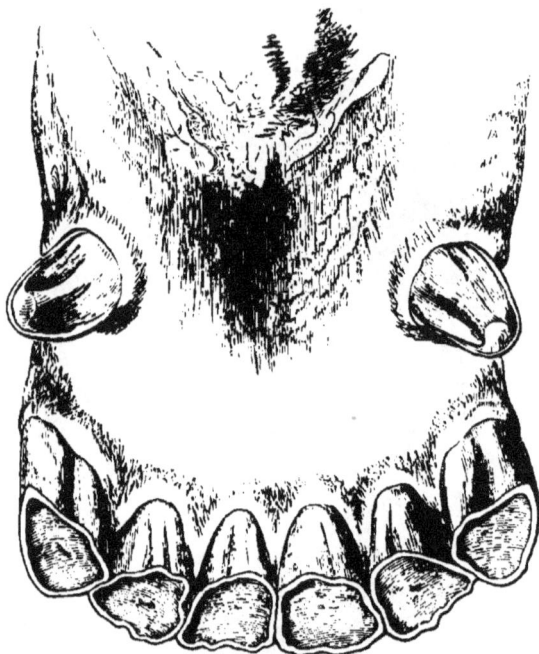

those of " Kremlin " seemed to have been worn as much as those of the older horse.

The central enamel can yet be seen in all the incisors of " Epirus " (Fig. 21). In fact, the remains of the marks are more evident than they are in the teeth of " Lothario " (Fig. 19) at twelve years of age. The tables of the incisors in the mouth of the older animal are triangular instead of square.

" Kremlin " (Fig. 20) shows a comparatively youthful form of the tables of the incisors, a condition which is due to the rectangular position of the teeth in regard to the jaw; but it is evident that the central enamel is entirely worn out, not a trace remaining. The small circles in the tables of the teeth merely indicate the apex of the inverted cone in which the infundibulum originally existed, and any good observer looking at the two mouths would decide that " Kremlin " was older than " Epirus." It is, however, quite certain that both horses were of the same age, and both of them much older than the teeth indicated them to be.

A method of judging the age of the horse up to thirty years, by noting the length of a groove in the upper corner incisors, is referred to by Mr. Sidney Galvayne in his pamphlet on horse dentition. The groove to which Mr. Galvayne attaches so much importance is really a groove in the fang of the upper corner

Fig. 22.—(a) *Groove at the side of the upper corner Incisor at ten years of age.*

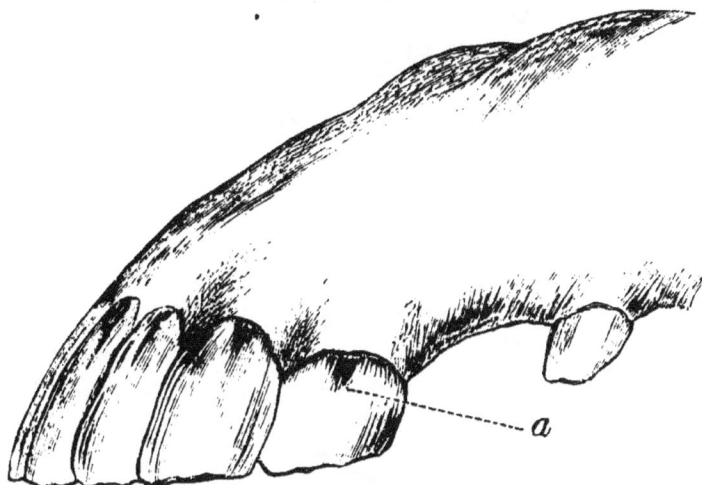

incisors. It is not seen until the horse has reached the age of ten years, by which time the alveolar cavity has become shallow, the tooth has grown in length in proportion to the wear, and a portion of the fang—with the lateral groove—is exposed. This appearance is shown in the above illustration (Fig. 22) from Mr. Galvayne's book.

According to the author, eleven years elapse before the lateral groove extends to the bottom of the tooth, and the age is to be judged during that time by the extension of the groove year by year. As the incisor is worn the fang grows longer, and the walls of the alveolar cavity are absorbed.

It is evident that the extension of the groove year by year

must be very gradual, and to distinguish the slight difference
between the groove of ten years and the groove of eleven years
is possible only to an expert who has devoted himself to the

Fig. 23.—(*b*) *Groove reaching half-way down the corner Incisor at
fifteen to sixteen years old.*

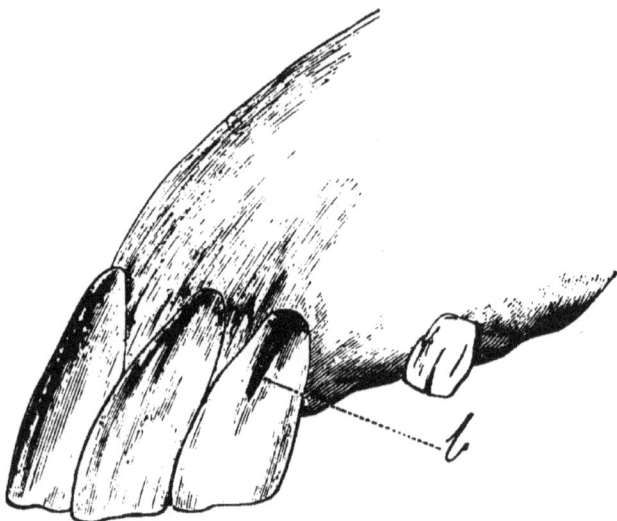

study of the subject, and has had numerous opportunities of
correcting his observations.

Fig. 24.—(*c*) *Groove extending the whole length of the corner Incisor
at twenty-one years old.*

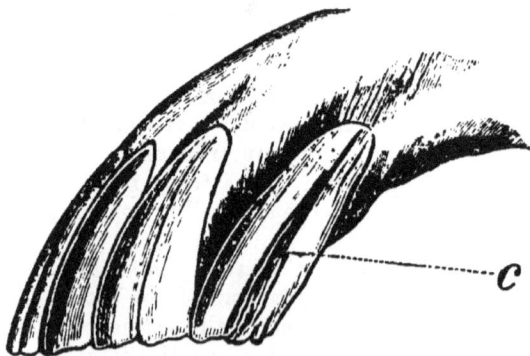

From the account which the originator of the system gives
of his successful attempts to define the exact ages of old horses
whose exact ages were known to his interrogators, the reader may

be satisfied that the test is a reliable one, and at the least it adds to the means of judging the age of the horse at a period when the signs on which reliance was formerly placed no longer exist.

Fig. 25.—(*d*) *Groove grown down from the gum, leaving the upper part of the tooth smooth at the age of twenty-six years.*

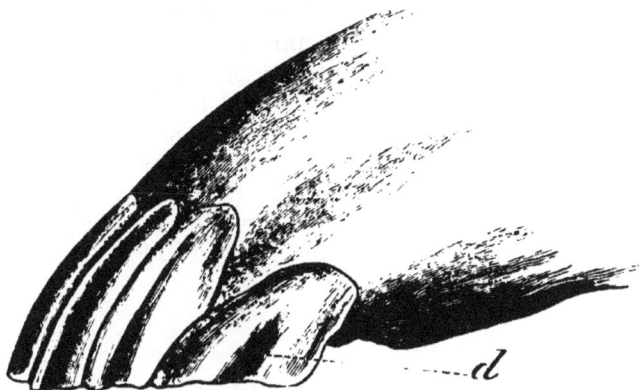

The drawing on p. 32 (Fig. 23) shows the groove about half-way down the tooth, which will indicate the age of fifteen or sixteen years.

Year by year the same process continues, and at twenty-one

Fig. 26.—(*e*) *Groove nearly worn out, upper part of Incisor round and smooth at thirty years old.*

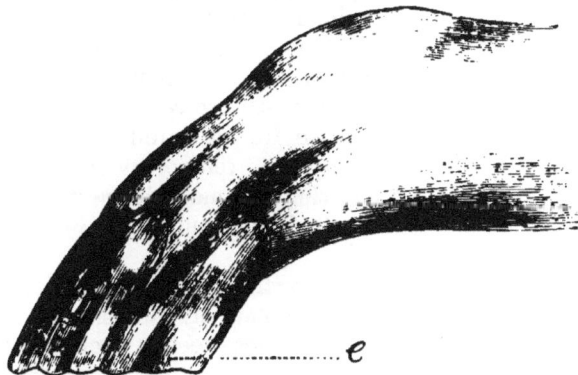

years of age the groove is seen along the entire surface of the corner incisor, as shown in the drawing (Fig. 24, opposite).

As the growth of the grooves of the tooth and wear of the

C

crown, added to the continued absorption of the alveolus, goes on, it follows that the groove will finally be worn out and the tooth be left round and smooth. Fig. 25 shows the upper part of the incisor next the gum in this condition, while the groove commences near the middle of the tooth.

By the age of thirty the groove is nearly worn out, only a small portion remaining at the bottom of the incisor, the whole of the upper part of the tooth being smooth.

The author of the system by long observation acquired great skill and accuracy in judging the ages of old horses, from ten years to thirty, but the stock-owner is not likely to devote enough time to the subject to master all the difficulties. He will, however, be interested to know that by an ingenious and comparatively simple method of observation the age of the horse may be judged up to an advanced period of life.

DENTITION OF THE OX.

In the front of the mouth of the ox there are eight incisors or cutting teeth in the lower jaw only. In the front of the upper jaw there is an elastic pad of fibrous tissue, covered with mucous membrane. The incisors may be distinguished as centrals, or first pair; middles, or second pair; laterals, or third pair; and corners, or fourth pair; the same terms being equally applicable to the temporary and permanent organs.

Temporary incisor teeth are easily distinguished from the permanent by their size. The fangs of the temporary teeth are much shorter than those of the permanent, but this fact is not to be recognised until the teeth are removed from the jaw. No question is likely to arise in the mind of the examiner as to the distinction between temporary and permanent organs in the ox; in fact, the common term "broad teeth," as applied to the latter, sufficiently indicates their prominent feature.

Molar teeth are named according to their position. In the temporary set there are three molars on each side of the upper and lower jaw, and in the adult these teeth are changed for permanent organs; while three additional teeth, the fourth, fifth, and sixth in position, all of which are permanent teeth from the first, are added, making the full set of permanent molar teeth six on each side of the upper and lower jaws.

From the illustration of the incisors of the ox, originally published in Girard's work and afterwards copied by Youatt and others, the reader would be led to believe that the temporary incisors were protruded into the mouth in pairs. Thus, at birth two teeth are shown standing up prominently from the gum. In the course of a fortnight two more are added, then two more,

Fig. 27.—*Incisors of Calf at birth.*

and at the end of a month or five weeks the eight teeth are well up. Nothing of this sort, however, occurs in nature; on the contrary, in the mouth of the *calf at birth*, the temporary teeth, molars, and incisors, are all so far advanced that they may be

Fig. 28.—*Incisors of Calf at one month.*

seen in outline under the gum, and commonly the cutting edges of the incisors and a few of the points of the molars are uncovered. The illustration above (Fig. 27) shows the state of the incisors at birth.

The advance of the teeth and the receding of the gums proceed very rapidly after birth, and at the age of *one month* the

Fig. 29.— *Molars of Calf at one month.*

T.M., temporary molars.

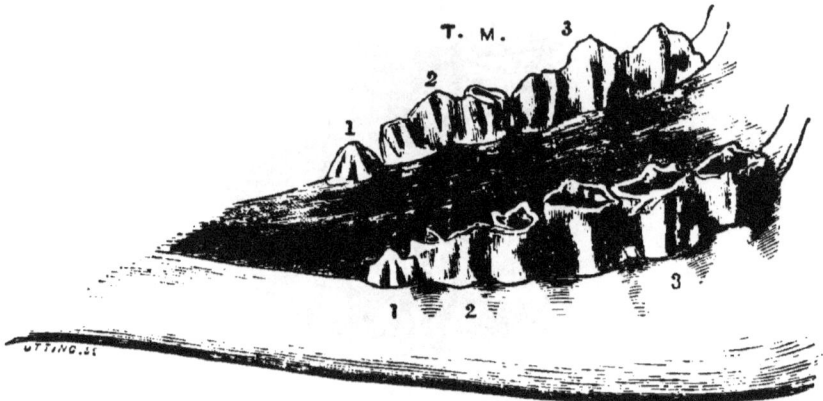

temporary teeth, viz. eight incisors in the lower jaw and three molars on each side in the top and bottom jaws, are fully

Fig. 30.— *Molars of Calf at six months.*

P.M., permanent molar.

developed. Figs. 28 and 29 show the temporary incisors and molars in the calf of one month old.

No accurate opinion of the age of a calf can be formed from

the observation of the state of the dentition between the ages of one and six months, when the fourth molar is cut ; but during this period the jaws expand, the incisor teeth gradually become less crowded, and the space between the third molar and the angle of the jaw increases as the fourth molar, which is the first permanent tooth, advances to occupy its place, as shown in Fig. 30.

At the age of *six months* the fourth molar is well developed, but it is in close contact with the angle of the jaw, and the posterior surface is not quite free from the covering of the gum.

Between six and twelve months old there are no important

Fig. 31. *Incisors of Steer at one year.*

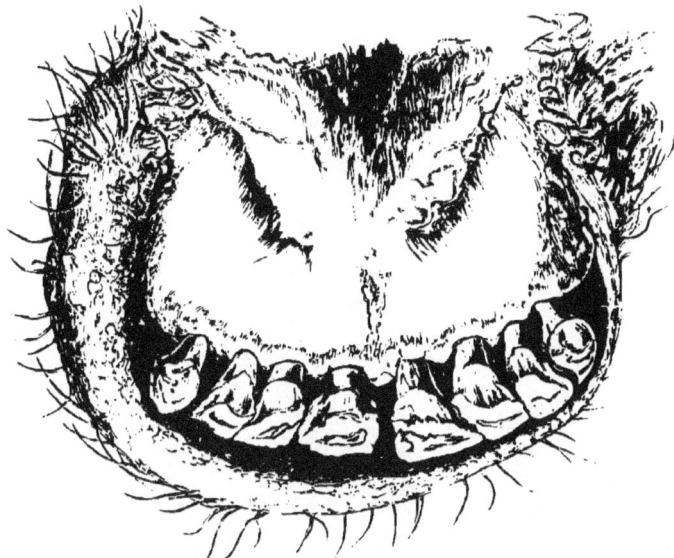

dental changes, the incisor teeth become worn, and as the jaws increase in size there is more space left between them ; but it is not possible to assert from the states of the incisor teeth whether an animal is under or over the age of one year.

The illustration above (Fig. 31) represents the average state of the incisors at the age of one year.

Shortly after one year the fifth molar begins to make its appearance, and at fifteen months it is well up. The appearance which the fifth molar presents at this age is very much like that of the fourth molar at the age of six months. The new tooth is in close contact with the angle of the jaw, and the gum covers the extreme posterior part of its surface. These appearances are shown in the illustration on next page (Fig. 32).

Fig. 32.—*Molars of Steer at fifteen months.*
P.M., permanent molars.

Fig. 33.—*Incisors of Heifer at one year and ten months.*

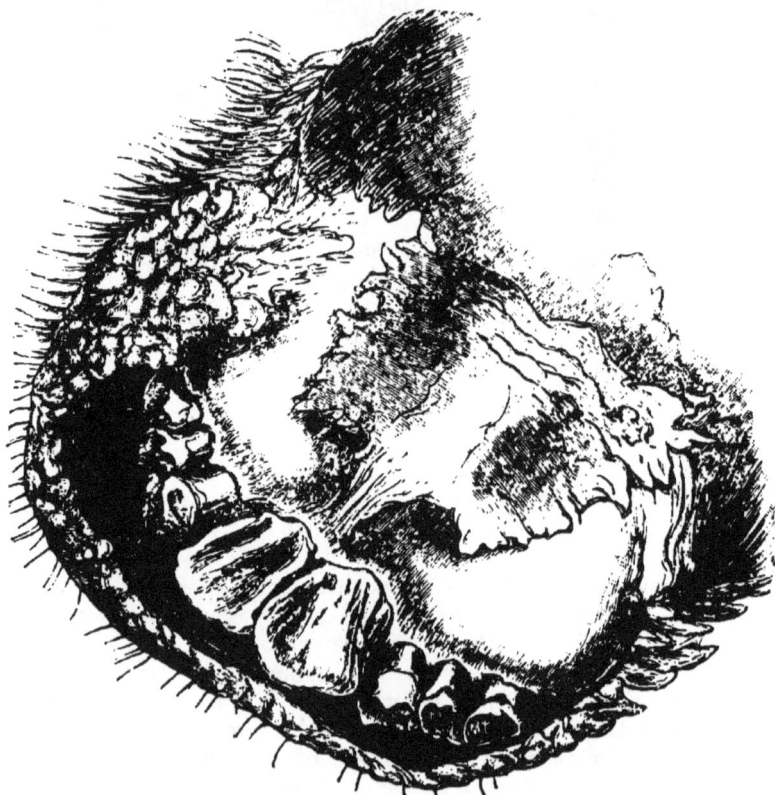

No change occurs in the incisors, excepting that which is caused by the wear of the teeth and the growth of the jaw, until the age of one year and eight or nine months, at which time the two central teeth become loose and the first broad teeth sometimes begin to project through the gum. In very forward animals the central permanent incisors are cut at the age of a year and seven months, but they are never level with the other incisors before one year and ten months, and their perfect development is indicative of the age of two years.

The illustration opposite (Fig. 33) was taken from a Shorthorn heifer at the age of *one year and ten months*, and may be accepted as indicative of the general appearance of the incisors at that age.

While the first pair of permanent incisors are advancing to

Fig. 34.—*Showing the sixth molar at two years.*

T.M., temporary molars.   P.M., permanent molars.

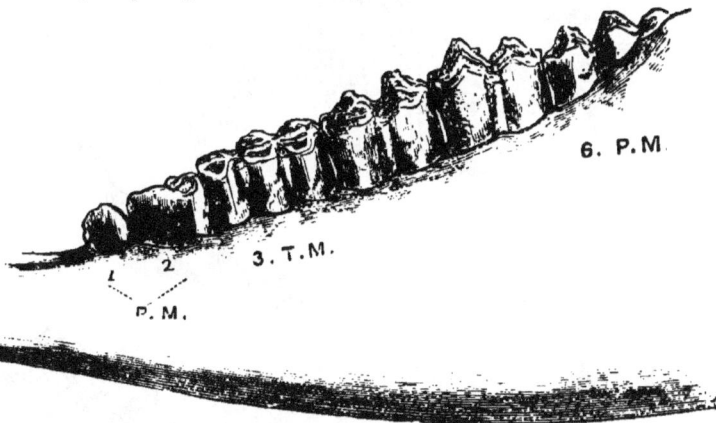

take the place of the temporary teeth, the sixth and last permanent molars push their way through the gum, and at the age of *two years* are in position. Any error of opinion as to the age which might arise from the premature cutting of the central permanent incisors may be corrected by reference to the state of the molars.

In the above illustration (Fig. 34) the sixth molar is shown in the position described, and in the same figure the first and second permanent molars have taken the places of the temporary teeth; this change, in the writer's experience, does not usually occur until the animal is a month or two over two years of age. Many cattle entered in the class not exceeding two years are certified to be one year and eleven months and two or three weeks old, and at this age the central broad teeth will be

well up ; but no signs of the cutting of the middle incisors are
to be seen, and when animals are exhibited in this class with
four broad teeth well developed, no hesitation need be felt in
certifying that the state of the dentition indicates the animal to
be above the stated age.

From *two years and two months* to *two years and six months*
the second pair of broad teeth, the middle permanent incisors,
are cut and occupy the place of the corresponding temporary
teeth in all the cultivated breeds. Instances of late dentition

Fig. 35.—*Incisors of Ox at two years and three months to two
years and six months.*

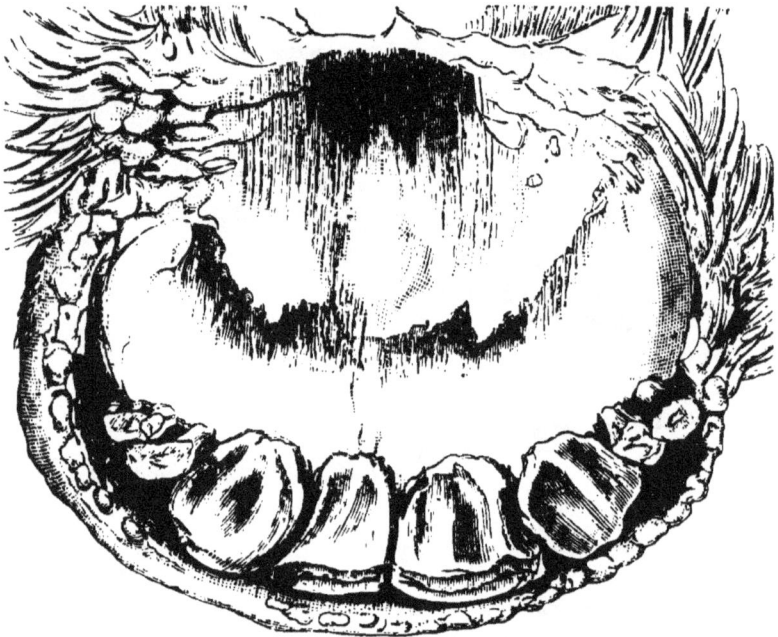

present themselves from time to time, in which the middle permanent incisors are not cut until the animal is approaching
three years old. There is consequently a possible variation of
several months in the time of the appearance of these teeth.

In the above illustration (Fig. 35) the ordinary condition of
the incisors at two years and six months is shown, but it is important to note that the incisors may present the same appearance
at two years and three months. Under these circumstances a
definite opinion can only be given after a careful examination of
the molar teeth.

At two years and two or three months the change of the

anterior temporary molars for permanent teeth will be going on. Some of the new teeth will be cut, but not fully grown, and

Fig. 36.—*Molars of Ox at three years.*

P.M., permanent molars.

several of the temporary organs still remain in their places. By two years and a half most of these will have given place to

Fig. 37.—*Incisors of Ox at two years and seven months to three years.*

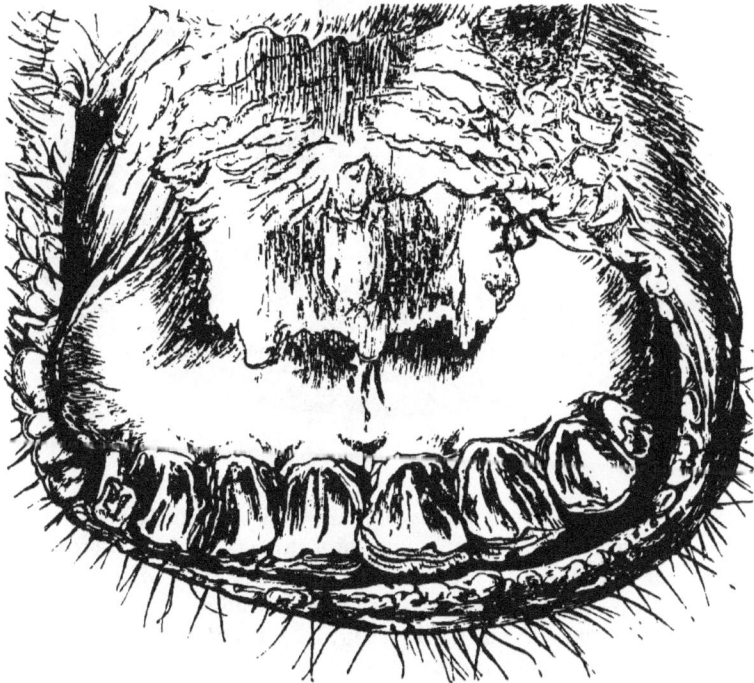

newly cut permanent teeth, and by two years and nine or ten months all the anterior temporary molars will have disappeared and the permanent teeth will occupy their places, and the animal at the age of *three years* will have the three anterior molars on each side the top and bottom jaws nearly level with the other teeth, but showing no signs of wear.

The illustration on p. 41 (Fig. 36) exhibits the three recently cut anterior molars as they appear when the ox is verging on three years of age.

The eruption of the third pair of permanent incisors may

Fig. 38.—*Incisors of Ox at two years and ten months to three years and three months.*

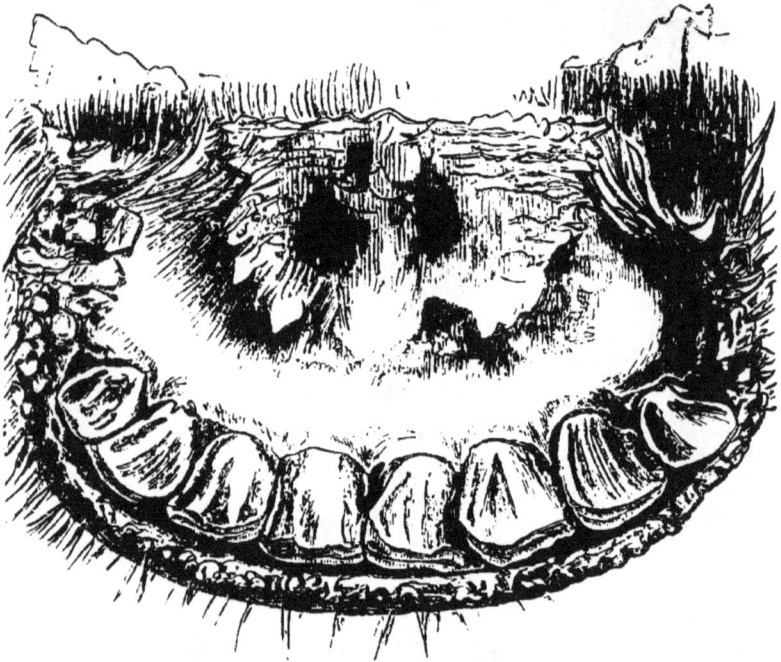

occur at any time between two years and six months and three years of age. These teeth are present, as a rule, before the animal is three years old, and occasionally they will be found well developed soon after two years and a half.

The illustration on p. 41 (Fig. 37) represents the average condition of the teeth at three years of age.

The fourth pair of broad teeth, the corner permanent incisors, are also subject to great variation in the time of cutting. They take the place of the temporary teeth soon after the eruption of the third pair, and they are frequently well developed at two

years and ten months old, while in some instances they are not
cut until three years and six months, or even later.

In the illustration opposite (Fig. 38), the state of the incisor
teeth in forward animals at *two years and ten months* is depicted.

The eruption of the corner permanent incisors, the fourth
pair of broad teeth, completes the permanent dentition of the
ox ; and from what has been stated in regard to irregular eruption of the corner teeth, an examiner will realise how necessary

Fig. 39.—*Incisors of Ox at five years.*

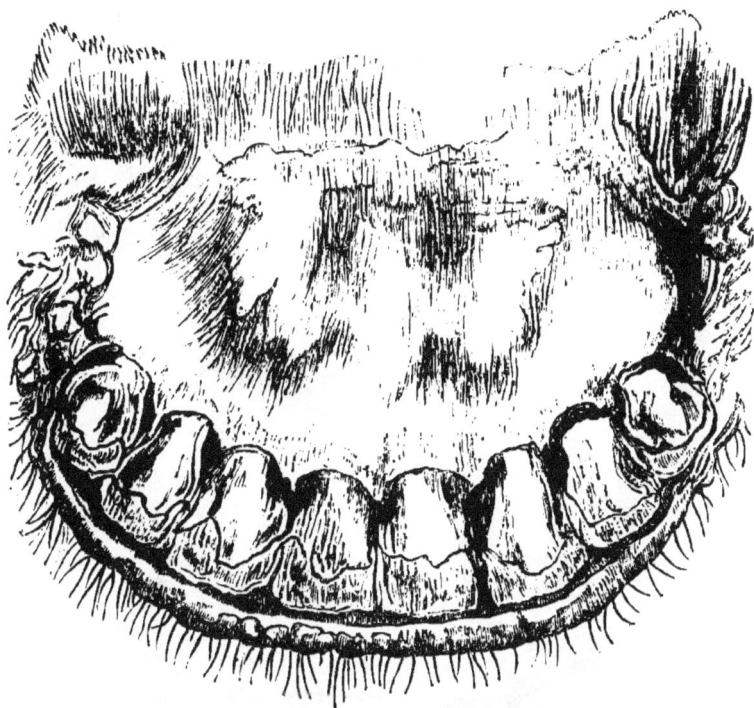

it is to be careful in judging an animal's age on the evidence
afforded by them.

After this period the changes in the form of the teeth which
are due to attrition will assist the expert in forming an
opinion of the age ; but no exact estimate can be based on such
evidence. The five-year-old ox (Fig. 39, above) will show a
considerable amount of worn surface in the central, middle, and
lateral incisors, and the cutting edge of the corner teeth will
be marked by a line of wear ; but no one would attempt

to determine whether or not an animal were under or above the age of five, and as the years increase the difficulty of judging the age by the appearance of the teeth is not diminished. It is not usually a matter of much importance to decide whether an ox is six years old or seven, and there are no well defined marks in the teeth which justify the examiner in giving an

Fig. 40.—*Incisors of Ox at ten years.*

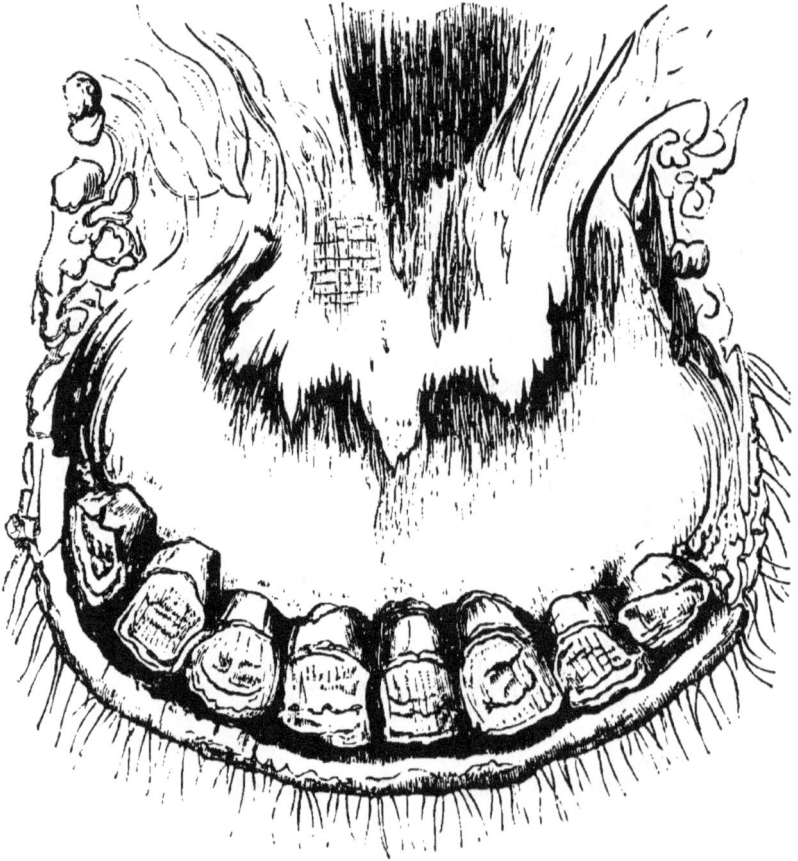

opinion as to the exact age which the animal has reached. Some evidence is afforded by the horns, which, although not perfectly reliable, may aid the expert in forming an opinion. The recognised rule is to add two to the number of rings at the base of the horn, the total representing the number of years of the animal's life. The teeth become narrower and more widely separated from each other year by year, and the worn surface much broader, as seen in the illustration opposite (Fig. 40), of the mouth of an ox at the age of ten years.

It will be seen that the characteristics of age are well exhibited in the above. But it is also evident that the changes in the teeth of the ox resulting from wear are not, as in the teeth of the horse, of so definite a character as to enable the expert to give an opinion up to an advanced period of the animal's life.

DENTITION OF THE SHEEP.

The terms which are applied to the teeth of the ox for the purpose of description may be used in regard to the teeth of the sheep. Eight incisors, central, lateral, middle, and corner teeth, are found in front of the lower jaw only, the corresponding part of the upper jaw being provided with an elastic pad, as in the ox. Molar teeth are designated by numbers, to indicate their position, and for the purpose of judging the age. These teeth

Fig. 41.—*Incisors of Lamb at birth.*

in the sheep may be described as corresponding to the teeth of the ox in all general points, except in regard to their size. *At birth*, the arrangement of the incisor teeth of the lamb is peculiar, as shown in Fig. 41.

Generally the whole temporary set of teeth may be recognised, but only in outline, as they are nearly covered with the gum. The central incisors are most advanced, and next in order come the laterals, leaving the middle and corner teeth considerably below them. Very often the cutting edges of the front and third pairs of teeth are through the gum. All these peculiarities are seen in the illustration, which may be accepted as a representation of the ordinary appearance of the teeth of the lamb at birth.

By the end of the *fourth week* all the temporary teeth, eight incisors, and three molars on each side of the upper and lower jaws, are well up.

From the time of the perfect eruption of the temporary teeth, at the age of one month, to the cutting of the first pair of broad teeth, central permanent incisors, at the age of one year to fifteen months, the only changes which will guide the expert to a correct opinion of the age are those which affect the molar teeth.

Fig. 42.—*Molars of Lamb at three months.*

. P.M., permanent molar.   T.M., temporary molars.

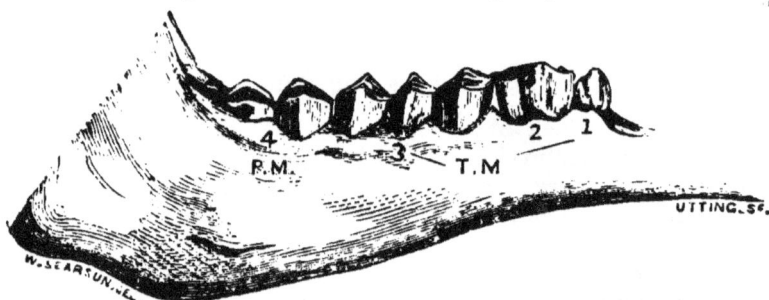

At *three months* the first permanent molar, the fourth in situation, is cut, and is recognised by its recent appearance in comparison with the tooth immediately in front of it, the third temporary molar, which shows signs of wear.

Fig. 43.—*Molars of Sheep at nine months.*

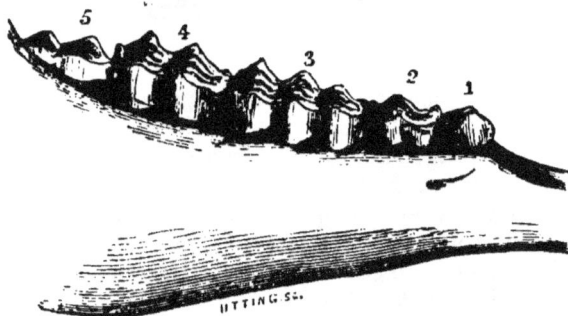

In the above illustration (Fig. 42) the appearance of the molars at the age of three months is shown.

During a period of five or six months from the cutting of the fourth molar there is nothing to guide the examiner except the growth of the teeth and of the jaw, which results in leaving a space behind the fourth molar.   At the age of *nine months* this space is occupied by the fifth molar, as shown in the drawing above (Fig. 43).

At *one year old* the teeth will present the following appearances. Incisors are worn on their upper surfaces, especially the central and middle, and to some extent the lateral teeth; the corners are not worn. In sheep which are feeding on turnips, some of the incisors, and in certain cases all of them,

Fig. 44.—*Incisors (temporary) of Sheep at one year.*

are broken off, and in very forward animals the central permanent incisors are cut, but they are never perfectly level and regular at this age.

Fig. 44 shows the average state of the temporary incisors in a well-preserved mouth at the age of one year. At the back of

Fig. 45.—*Incisors of Sheep, central permanent Incisors well up, at fifteen months.*

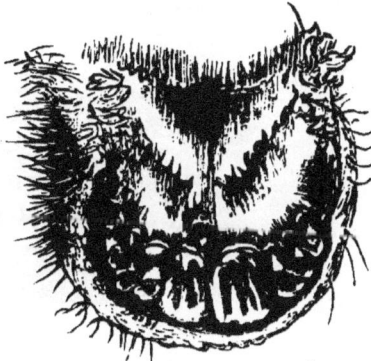

the mouth the recently cut fifth permanent molar is seen, while the teeth in front of it are all worn on the surfaces; these appearances, taken in connection with the state of the incisors, will satisfy the examiner that the sheep is about the age of one year.

The first broad teeth, central incisors, are usually cut soon after one year old, and are well up at *fifteen months*, as shown in the last illustration (Fig. 45).

Fig. 46.—*Incisors of Sheep, second pair of permanent Incisors cut (four broad teeth), at one year and ten months.*

At *eighteen months* the sixth permanent molar is cut, and the recent appearance which this tooth presents is better evidence of this age than can be obtained by an inspection of the incisors. Occasionally in very forward mouths the second pair of broad teeth will be cut; in other cases there will be no signs

Fig. 47.— *Molars of Sheep at one year and ten months.*

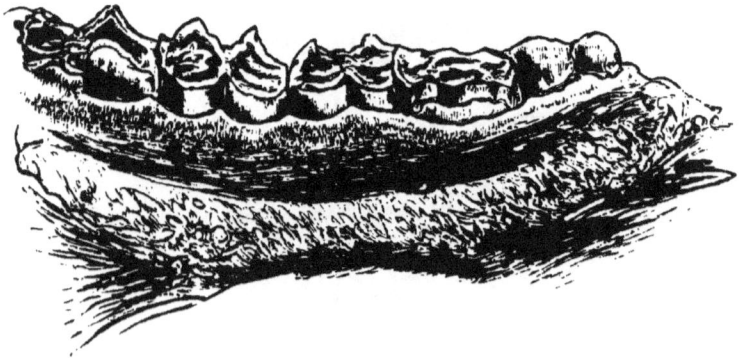

of their appearance until the sheep is approaching the age of two years (see Fig. 46, which shows the second pair of broad teeth at the age of one year and ten months). So far, therefore, as these teeth are concerned, the examiner may be left in doubt as to whether the sheep is one year and six months or two years old, and it is absolutely necessary that he should inspect the molars, in which important changes occur between the ages of fifteen months and two years.

Soon after the sheep reaches *one year and a half,* the sixth molar begins to protrude through the gum. Shortly afterwards the two anterior temporary molars give place to the permanent teeth, and the third temporary molar is a mere shell covering the top of the permanent tooth, which is coming up beneath it, and pushing it out of its place, as shown in the last illustration (Fig. 47).

In this drawing the average condition of the molars of the sheep just under *two years* is exhibited. The two anterior permanent molars are cut, the third permanent molar is coming up under the temporary tooth, which in many cases will have fallen out, leaving the permanent organ to be seen below the

Fig. 48.—*Six broad teeth at two years and three months.*

level of the other teeth. At the back of the jaw the sixth molar is seen, but does not show any marks of wear, and this tooth, it may be observed, affords the most valuable evidence at a critical period. In the class " not exceeding two years," many of the sheep are stated to be twenty months old, and some of the animals may have the third pair of broad teeth not fully developed, but fairly advanced. When sheep exhibited as under two years of age are found to have six broad teeth the animals are naturally objects of suspicion, and further evidence is sought for in the molars, which, as the drawing (Fig. 47) shows, exhibit very characteristic marks at this period. Generally it may be taken as a fact that if a sheep with six broad teeth shows the three anterior molars in a state which proves that they are recently cut, and especially if one or more of the temporary teeth still remain, the age does not exceed two years.

D

Six broad teeth well up may generally be taken to indicate that the sheep is *two years and three months* (Fig. 48), but in many animals they are not present until two years and a half. On the other hand, they are not uncommonly cut at twenty-two months old, a fact which was recorded by the writer more than thirty years ago, and since then they have been met with at twenty months.

In any instance of such exceptional dentition being found in sheep entered in the class not exceeding two years, it will be necessary to inspect the molars. If the three anterior molars and the sixth molar present evidence of having been only recently cut, and especially if one or more of the temporary

Fig. 49.—*Incisors of Sheep at three years old, showing recently cut corner teeth.*

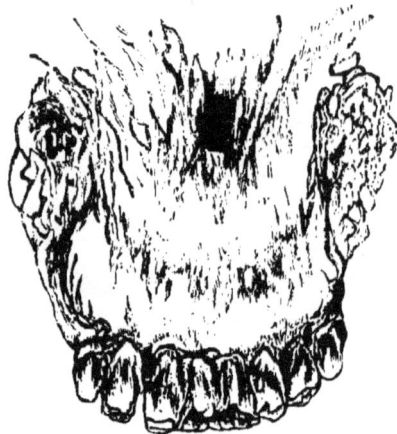

molars remain, the cutting of the third pair of broad teeth will not justify disqualification. Should, however, the molar teeth exhibit a uniform character, all their surfaces being quite level, it may be concluded that the sheep is over two years of age.

Dentition in sheep is completed by the eruption of the corner permanent incisors, which are usually cut at the age of three years, as shown in the above drawing.

In some cases the corner teeth are not well up till the animal is nearly four years old, so that there is a possibility of a mistake being made as to the age to the extent of a year, by an examiner who contents himself with an inspection of the corner incisors. No difficulty, however, would be experienced in deciding whether the corner incisors represent three years or four years, if the state of the other incisors is taken into account. At four years of age the six broad teeth will show marks of

wear; the central incisors especially will be worn hollow on their
upper surfaces, the middles and laterals also showing well-
marked tables in the place of sharp cutting edges; while the
recently cut corner incisors, supposing their eruption to have
been delayed till the sheep was nearly four years old, will present a marked contrast to the rest of the teeth which have
suffered from attrition. These appearances are shown in the
next drawing (Fig. 50) of the mouth of a sheep at the age of
four years.

Fig. 50.—*Incisors of Sheep at four years*

After the age of four years, and indeed from the time of the
completion of permanent dentition, whether early or late, the
changes which are effected in the form of the incisors by wear
vary according to the nature of the food, and the examiner must
be content to limit his inquiries to the period within which is
comprised the eruption of the permanent teeth.

DENTITION OF THE PIG.

When dentition is perfect, the pig has six incisor teeth in
the front of both upper and lower jaw—two central, two lateral,
and two corner teeth. Behind the corner teeth are the tusks,
one on each side, in the upper and lower jaws. Between the
tusks and the molar teeth there are usually four small teeth
which are described as pre-molars, one on each side of both jaws,
and twenty-four molars, six on each side of the upper and lower
jaws.

Temporary and permanent incisors agree generally in number,
form, and position, but the temporary molars are only three
in number on each side of the upper and lower jaws, and the
third molar has three cusps instead of two. The temporary

tusks are much smaller and more pointed than the permanent teeth which replace them, and the pre-molars are not represented by temporary teeth, but are permanent from the first.

It may be observed that no difficulty is found by the experts in distinguishing the permanent incisors from the temporary

Fig. 51.—*Teeth of Pig at birth.*

organs, especially when both orders are in the mouth together. The distinction is not, however, so marked as to secure the tyro from risk of error.

At birth (Fig. 51), the pig has two sharp-pointed teeth laterally

Fig. 52.—*Incisors and Molars of Pig at one month.*

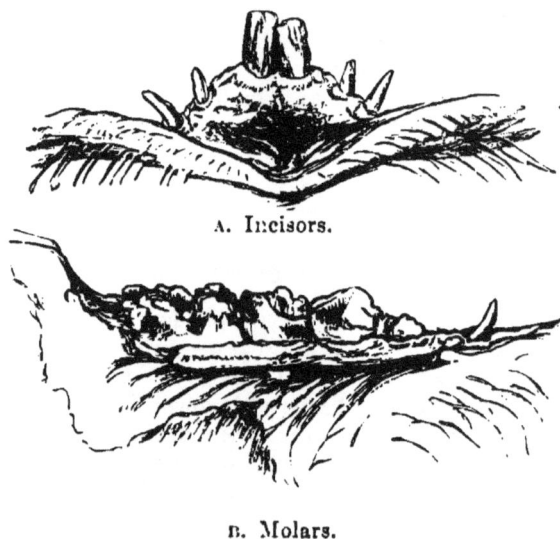

A. Incisors.

B. Molars.

placed in each jaw, top and bottom, leaving an open space in the front of the mouth (Fig. 51). The teeth much resemble small tusks; they are really the temporary tusk and corner incisors. No other teeth are in the mouth at the time of birth; but the temporary molars are immediately under the gum, and in the dried specimen they can be distinctly seen in their relative positions.

At *one month* old the three temporary molars on each side of the jaw, top and bottom, are cut, the second and third in position being well up, the first one just appearing through the gum; at the same time the two central temporary incisors in each jaw are cut, as shown in the illustration opposite (Fig. 52).

At *two months* old the temporary central incisors are fully

Fig. 53.—*Incisors and Molars of Pig at three months.*

A. Incisors.

B. Molars.

developed, and there are signs of the eruption of the lateral temporary incisors, which generally pierce the gums soon after two months. The first temporary molar is now nearly level with the second.

At *three months* old the pig has the temporary set of teeth fully developed, the lateral incisors by this time being nearly level with the centrals. The temporary corner teeth and the tusks are further removed from each other than they were at

birth, owing to the growth of the jaw. In Fig. 53 (p. 53) the
state of the teeth at three months old is indicated.

Excepting the natural growth of the jaws, in common with
other parts, no changes occur which will assist the examiner
in judging the age of the young pig until the age of *five months*
is reached. At this time there are evident signs of the cutting
of the pre-molars ; and the fourth molar, which is the first permanent tooth, is seen behind the temporary teeth.

The illustration below (Fig. 54) shows the state of the
molars at the age of *six months*.

As a large number of pigs are entered at Agricultural
Exhibitions at the age of between five and six months, it is
necessary to devote particular attention to the signs which are
exhibited by the teeth of the pig at this period ; and the inspector is particularly required to remember that the animal

Fig. 54.—*Molars of Pig at six months.*

which he is inspecting may be actually over the stated age at
the time of inspection, without, in consequence, being liable to
disqualification. This condition of things constantly occurs at
the Shows which are held after the date up to which the ages
are calculated ; it is obviously necessary to add the days or
weeks which have elapsed to the animal's certified age, at the
time of making the examination : for example, in cases where
ages are calculated to the 1st of June, while the Show takes
place early in July, a pig which is certified to be five months
three weeks and five days old in the class for animals not
exceeding six months, will be more than a month over the
certified age when it is seen by the inspector.

Again, it must be noted that the pre-molars are not always
developed, and in the same litter one or two pigs will be found
occasionally in which this tooth is absent. The fourth molar
is, however, remarkably regular in its appearance, and may be

referred to for the purpose of solving any doubt which may arise in consequence of the absence of the pre-molars.

Disqualification of a pig or pigs entered as not exceeding six months would occur under such circumstances as the following. The inspector, it may be supposed, is examining the teeth of a pig which is entered as five months and two days; he adds the weeks which have elapsed since the date up to which the age is calculated, and deals with the animal as having arrived at the age of six months and nine days. At this period he expects to find the pre-molars and the fourth molar well up, the fourth molar being close to the angle of the jaw, and scarcely free from the covering of gum at the extreme posterior part. But if the fourth molar stands out from the angle of the jaw, leaving space behind it, and if he observes in addition that the temporary corners have been changed for permanents, he does not hesitate to assert that the pig is at least a month older than it is certified to be. In some pigs the corner permanents are found with their points through the gum at *seven months,* but in many cases the temporary organs remain till the animal has reached the age of *eight months.*

Disqualifications in the six-month-old class are often very numerous; the pigs are shown as close to the age as possible, and the frequent presence of the corner teeth in pigs belonging to certain exhibitors is the cause of the animals being rejected.

Fig. 55.—*Molars of Pig at nine months.*

At *nine months* the corner permanent teeth are well up, and the permanent tusks may be through the gum in very forward animals at this age. In looking over the notes of the inspections which have been made for many years past, it is shown that, as a rule, the pig at the age of nine months has one or two of the temporary tusks still in position; in fact, the presence of well-developed permanent tusks in a pig entered as not exceeding nine months would be a fair ground of disqualification. The drawings (Figs. 55 and 56) show the state of the teeth at nine months.

A class for pigs not exceeding nine months of age at many Shows takes the place of the six-months' class, and therefore includes pigs of various ages from two or three months to over eight months. Disqualifications in this class generally affect pigs which are really under nine months, in which the state of the dentition indicates the age to be above that which is stated in the certificate. If, for instance, a pig which is entered in

Fig. 56.—*Temporary Incisors and Tusks of Pig at nine months.*

this class as five months and two weeks has the corner teeth just cut, or one entered as six months and twenty-one days shows evidence of the changing of the temporary tusks, in these cases no hesitation is felt in disqualifying the animals, although in both cases the animals are below the limit of age in the class in which they are entered.

One year old is the age when, according to received opinions, the central permanent incisors are cut. It is, however, more often seen that the temporary incisors are still in their places in pigs which are just under the age of one year; and although the permanent teeth, when cut, advance very rapidly, a pig entered as not exceeding one year would be looked upon with

much suspicion if the central permanent incisors were found to
be cut; and if they were well up and some of the anterior temporary molars had fallen, and the permanent teeth were filling their
places, the animal would be disqualified.

The fifth molar tooth is always cut between ten and twelve
months, and its perfect eruption may be taken as evidence that

Fig. 57.—*Central permanent Incisors and Tusks of Pig at one year*
(Early dentition).

the pig has reached the age of one year. In the above illustration
(Fig. 57) the recently cut central incisors are shown; a state of
dentition which is seen only in very forward animals at the completion of one year of age.

Shortly after the completion of one year, the three anterior
temporary molars fall irregularly; and by the time the animal

is fifteen months old the three anterior permanent molars
are in the mouth, and may readily be known by their sharp
unworn points and their recent appearance, as shown in the
next illustration (Fig. 58).   These teeth are very regular in their

Fig. 58.—*Teeth of Pig at fifteen months ; the three permanent
anterior Molars recently cut.*

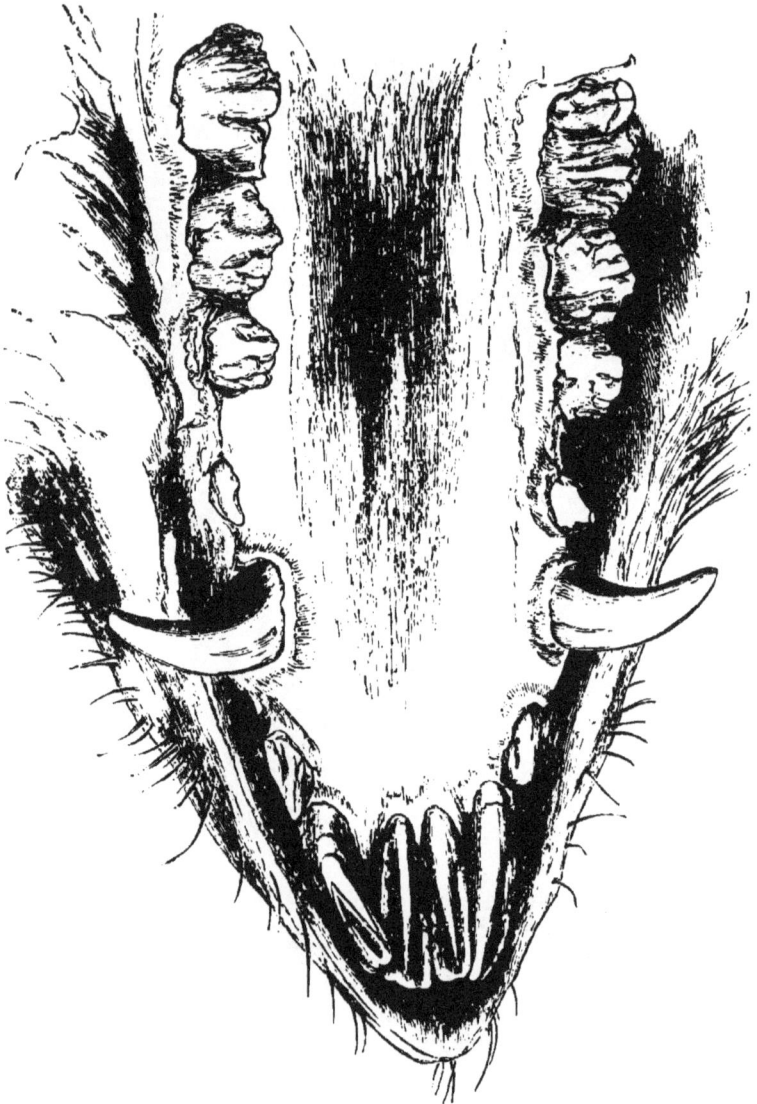

development, and afford valuable evidence in cases where an opinion cannot be formed from an inspection of the incisors alone.

The next change in the dentition is the final one, and occurs between the age of *seventeen and eighteen months.* At this period the sixth molar, a permanent tooth, is cut; and in forward animals the lateral temporary incisors are changed for permanent teeth. In many instances the temporary lateral teeth remain up to the age of eighteen months, although they are in such cases quite loose; and very often the permanent teeth are cutting through the gum below or by the side of them; in other instances one lateral is found to be fully up and nearly level with the centrals, while the other is just pushing through the gum. The sixth molar is also fairly up, but the posterior part of its crown is not quite clear from the gum.

These changes complete the permanent dentition of the pig, and there are no indications of the age afforded by the teeth

Fig. 59.—*Molars of Pig at eighteen months, sixth Molar well up.*

after this period, excepting such as depend on the growth and wear of the organs.

In the above illustration (Fig. 59) the sixth molar is shown as it appears at the completion of the age of *eighteen months.*

It is very important that the examiner should exercise the greatest care in the inspection of the teeth of pigs which are exhibited in the class above twelve and not exceeding eighteen months old. Animals are entered at various ages from twelve to eighteen months; it is necessary, therefore, in this class to note the condition of the central incisors and the anterior molars, as well as that of the lateral incisors and the sixth molar. In the next drawing (Fig. 60, p. 60) the full development of the lateral permanent incisors is shown. This state of dentition, it may be remarked, is indicative of a year and eight months.

At the age of two years the lateral permanent incisors are quite level with the centrals and are worn on their edges, the

sixth molar now stands quite free from contact with the angle
of the jaw, and indications of wear may be observed on the

Fig. 60.—*Incisors and Tusks of Pig at one year and eight months;
lateral permanent Incisors well up.*

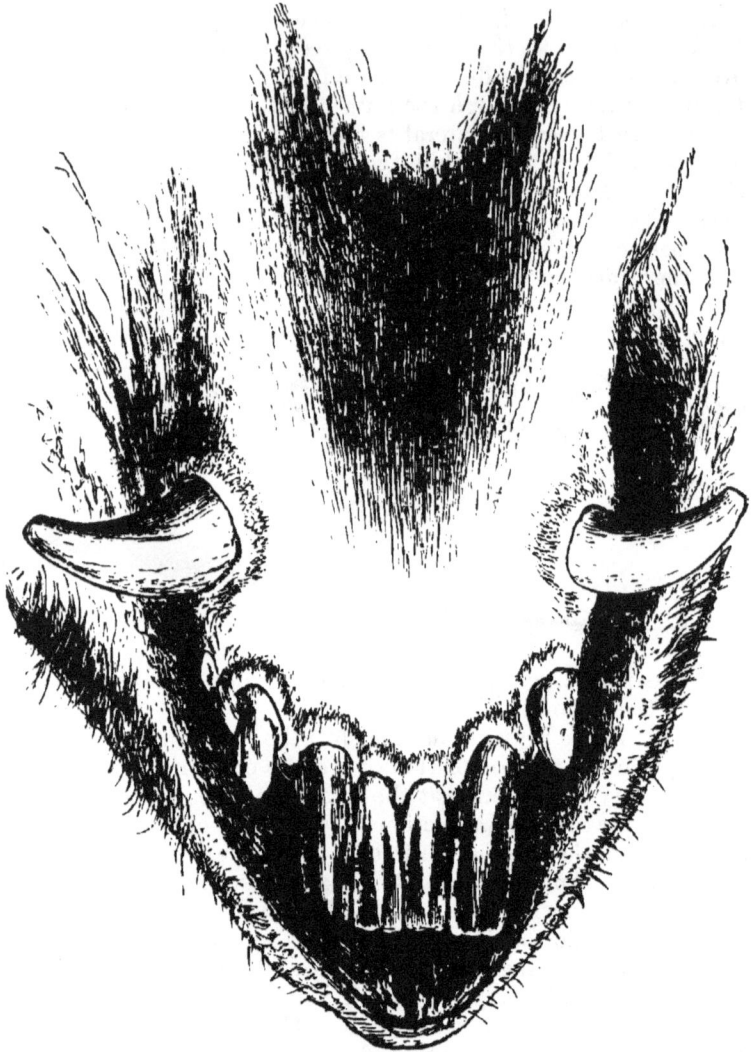

upper surface of the other molars.   After the pig has attained
the age of two years, an opinion as to the age must be to a great
extent speculative.   The wear which the teeth undergo, the

darkening of their colour, and the growth of the tusks, will afford some evidence which will assist the judgment; but there are no changes which can be referred to as indicative of the exact age of the pig after the lateral incisors and the sixth molars are fully developed.

In the course of the above remarks on the changes which occur in the teeth of the pig at different ages, certain exceptions to the rule of development have been mentioned; they are not numerous, nor very important in their bearings, and it is a subject of common remark that the exceptions are nearly always in favour of the exhibitor, being in the direction of retarded rather than accelerated development.

It may be useful to say a final word in reference to a common mistake into which exhibitors, or rather their servants, frequently fall, *i.e.* the error of believing that a little discrepancy between the state of dentition and the certified age of an animal is not of much consequence so long as the age does not exceed the limit of the class in which the animal is entered. The teeth are inspected with the view to ascertain if they agree with the statement of the age in the certificate of entry, and not for the purpose of insuring that the animal is within the age to which the class is limited.

PRINTED BY
SPOTTISWOODE AND CO., NEW-STREET SQUARE
LONDON

www.ingramcontent.com/pod-product-compliance
Lightning Source LLC
Chambersburg PA
CBHW022027080426
42733CB00007B/757